Creative Cross-Pollination

CREATIVE
CROSS-POLLINATION

A Former Imagineer's Take on the Innovation Process

BRIAN COLLINS
ILLUSTRATED BY NICOLA GIGANTE

RIVERSHORE
PRESS

ISBN: 978-1-960881-07-6

Cover design by Nicola Gigante
Illustrations by Nicola Gigante
Book design by Barry R. Hill

CONTENTS

Introduction

Why are you picking up this book? Perhaps you're a young professional, or a seasoned executive, or a busy entrepreneur and are looking for ways to spark some innovative thinking, either within yourself or amongst a group. The creative well has run dry and you're looking for a boost. Maybe you're a sales rep and are looking for some new techniques to generate more leads. Or you're a student with a big paper or project due and just can't get a grip on where to even start that crazy assignment. Well then, you've come to the right place — using Creative Cross-Pollination to spark your innovation can certainly help you, and in a big way. But you're the more obvious ones. I'm hoping that some of the following people are also out there flipping through this book:

Doctors: Surgeons researching a new surgical technique or solution? Orthopedists trying to develop a new splint?

Soldiers: Warfighters who need new field solutions? Officers that need innovative training techniques?

Actors: Need ideas for developing a character's traits?

The Unemployed (or under-employed): Looking to explore new ways to apply your skill set?

First Responders, Architects, Engineers, Artists, Teachers, Moms . . .

I could go on and on, but hopefully you get the idea.

If you are looking for a creative solution, a new perspective, or have a problem to solve, Creative Cross-Pollination can work for you. If you have a need or have been asked to facilitate a brainstorming session, Creative Cross-Pollination can work for you. If you're just stuck in a rut and are looking for a way out . . . Creative Cross-Pollination can work for you.

Before I get too deep into this book, though, one thing that I'd like to make clear is that I didn't invent this technique. Mother Nature did. I'm just giving it a name and some prominence. As my first chapter explains, Creative Cross-Pollination has been with the human race since the beginning of time. Not only that, but I would go so far as to say it is a truly innate behavior, not only in humans, but for many sentient species. This means every one of us engages in this technique all the time and probably doesn't even realize they're doing it.

I don't believe I was aware I was using this concept when working at Imagineering. It wasn't until later in my career when, as a college instructor, I began to study some of the most talented individuals and respected organizations and explore the creative process and techniques which drove them to the highest levels of success. Amongst all the different techniques, styles, and personalities, the concept of what I've come to call *Creative Cross-Pollination* began to manifest itself over and over again. I found it to be a key and fundamental piece of the "innovation tool kit" that every one of us carries around.

My goal, then, is to raise your awareness of what Creative Cross-Pollination is and how to harness it as a powerful idea-generating technique. The techniques in this book are just the start. Once you become aware of what Creative Cross-Pollination is and master the basic principles, you'll find new ways to consciously leverage this skill and apply it to a wide variety of situations.

Ready to get started? We'll take a quick look at what Creative Cross-Pollination is, as well as explore what drives your "creative essence." After that, I've got four great techniques you can use to get started generating those new ideas.

Okay, then—let's get going.

Of
Birds
and
Bees

"You see things; and you say 'Why?'
But I dream things that never were; and I say 'Why not?'"

—George Bernard Shaw

Let's talk about the birds and the bees. Okay, not *that* talk—a different talk. Actually, let's drop the birds and just stick with the bees. Bees are wonderfully efficient and organized creatures. They live in complex social groups, are constantly busy (busy as bees . . .), and are terrific at one of the primary tasks that Mother Nature has laid out for them: cross-pollinating plants.

Think about a moment in your life when you connected two seemingly unrelated ideas. Maybe you were trying to solve a problem at work and thought about an unrelated hobby that unexpectedly inspired a solution. This is the essence of Creative Cross-Pollination: finding hidden connections that lead to innovation. Bees, for instance, are nature's experts at such a process. Their work ensures that ecosystems thrive and plants propagate, an interconnection that embodies how different worlds can support one another.

According to Webster's New World College Dictionary, *cross-pollination* is defined as "the transfer of pollen from the anther of one flower to the stigma of another with a different genetic composition, as by insects, or deliberately by a botanist." That's a complex scientific definition, but one with which most are familiar. In a broader context, especially or particularly within the business world, cross-pollination can be thought of as "the transfer of characteristics from one context to another with a different intent, either subconsciously or deliberately." In other words, finding a way to put a square peg in a round hole. Creative Cross-Pollination takes this concept and focuses it a little more. With

Creative Cross-Pollination we are looking for a *new* way to put a square peg in a round hole.

That "new" part is important. That's what elevates it to Creative Cross-Pollination. Dr. Teresa Amabile of Harvard Business School says that "A product or response will be judged as creative to the extent that (a) it is both a novel and appropriate, useful, correct, or valuable response to the task at hand, and (b) the task is heuristic rather than algorithmic."[1] This is one of my favorite definitions of creativity, and if you break it down, you'll see why—it's really not as academic as it sounds.

> A product or response will be judged as creative to the extent that (a) it is both a novel (new) and appropriate (there is a method to the madness), useful (it has a purpose), correct, or valuable response to the task at hand, and (b) the task is heuristic (taking the "scenic route" to get from point A to point B, allowing your mind to be open to new possibilities and letting your thought process diverge off the original path) rather than algorithmic (getting from point A to point B in a straightforward, linear fashion).

For something to be creative, then, your thought process must be heuristic—open to new ideas and allowing one to go on a journey of discovery. When we are engaged in Creative Cross-Pollination, we are taking that heuristic journey to find a new and appropriate solution to the task at hand by transferring characteristics from one context to another with a different intent, either subconsciously or deliberately.

In simpler terms, creativity thrives when there is both novelty and utility, but also when exploration leads us down paths that might not initially seem logical. Think of it as taking a stroll through a forest without a fixed route — you might stumble upon a beautiful clearing or discover a new path that reveals more than what a straightforward road ever could.

When we are engaged in Creative Cross-Pollination, we are taking that heuristic journey to find a new and appropriate solution to the task at hand by transferring characteristics from one context to another with a different intent, either subconsciously or deliberately.

Consider the creative minds behind famous innovations. The Wright brothers, for instance, used observations of bird flight to inform their design of the first successful airplane. Leonardo da Vinci studied the natural world meticulously, drawing parallels between bird anatomy and early flying machines. These pioneers didn't just think within the confines of one discipline; they looked outward at the same thing — birds — and merged ideas from biology, engineering, and art to create something extraordinary.

Now — let's take a closer look at Creative Cross-Pollination!

What is Creative Cross-Pollination?

So, what exactly is Creative Cross-Pollination and when did this concept originate? Well, one thing I can tell you is that I'm not going to take credit for coming up with this concept. That's because Creative Cross-Pollination is an innate method we all have for coming up with new ideas—each one of us does it naturally, whether we know it or not. Given this, Creative Cross-Pollination is probably as old as humankind itself, going all the way back to when our ancestors were still painting on cave walls and discovering fire for the first time.

Think about it. When our distant cousin Ug wanted to communicate his heroic hunting escapades, he couldn't just text his tribe back at camp or shoot off an email. He knew he wanted to communicate with nice pictures, maybe even color pictures. But therein was another problem. He could not run down to the nearest store and pick up paints or markers; best I can tell, they weren't around in Neanderthal days.

So—how was our friend Ug going to get color pictures on the walls of his cave? My best guess is that he remembered how the berries he ate stained his hands red or blue. Or perhaps he remembered how the clay in his cave town turned his feet burnt orange. We can't be exactly sure what caused his prehistoric light bulb to illuminate, but we do know that Ug (and many of his kind) did indeed use the things he found in nature to paint on his walls. Berry juice for paint—that's an ancient form of Creative Cross-Pollination. And ever since then, Creative Cross-Pollination has endured and manifested itself throughout history in many different facets.

Another flavor of Creative Cross-Pollination would be to think of Edward de Bono's definition of lateral thinking. Let me back up for a second and explain that de Bono divides thinking into two methods. The first is called "vertical thinking," which uses processes of logic and could be considered more algorithmic in style. "Lateral thinking" involves disrupting the apparent thought process and arriving at the solution from an unexpected heuristic angle.

Lateral thinking seeks to solve problems by apparently illogical means and requires individuals to look at things in a different way. Another way to say that would be it requires individuals to look at things in a creative way. *Resourcefulness* is a great term to describe Creative Cross-Pollination.

As Imagineers, we often sought solutions to our creative challenges by exploring ideas that would normally be ignored by "logical" thinking. As a matter of fact, if you've ever been part of a formal brainstorming session, one of the universal rules is that "no idea is a bad idea." Everything has merit and could be the seed to finding a solution, no matter how outrageous or improbable it might seem at the time. It's all about putting as many dots on the table as possible so at some point in the future you might be able to connect them. Steve Jobs, cofounder of Apple Computer, Inc., once said in his now-famous commencement address to Stanford University graduates:

> ". . . You can't connect the dots looking forward. You can only connect them looking backwards, so you have to trust that the dots will somehow connect in your future. You have to trust in something: your gut, destiny, life, karma, whatever. This approach has never let me down, and it has made all the difference in my life."

Creative Cross-Pollination has much to do with trusting that the "dots" you collect throughout your life will somehow connect in the future. It's often amazing how they do.

Summary

This chapter introduces the concept of Creative Cross-Pollination, drawing an analogy to how bees naturally cross-pollinate flowers to promote growth and diversity in nature. In business and personal development, Creative Cross-Pollination is about merging ideas from different areas to create novel solutions. The chapter underscores the importance of embracing new perspectives and explains how creativity requires an openness to exploring unconventional connections. Readers are encouraged to take a heuristic approach, where discovery happens by exploring a "scenic route" of ideas.

Exercises

Try this now

Think of a current project or problem you're working on. Take five minutes to brainstorm at least three unrelated areas that might offer insight or solutions.

Try these soon

Explore an interest or hobby outside your primary field of study. Write down any connections you observe with your main area of focus.

Identify a task you often complete in a routine way. List out a few alternative approaches you could try and consider any unexpected insights.

Create a "mind map" where you link an idea or project with five completely different fields. Draw lines to show how these areas could contribute to a unique solution.

Discussion Questions

1. How does the concept of cross-pollination apply to problem-solving in everyday life?

2. Why is it important to look beyond traditional methods when approaching challenges?

3. How does heuristic thinking contribute to creativity compared with algorithmic thinking?

4. Can you identify a real-life example where Creative Cross-Pollination led to a breakthrough?

5. How does Creative Cross-Pollination impact collaboration among team members from different backgrounds?

Your Mental Filing Cabinet

"I am enough of an artist to draw freely upon my imagination.
Imagination is more important than knowledge.
Knowledge is limited. Imagination encircles the world."

—Albert Einstein

It's been my experience that creative people tend to be pack rats—physically and mentally. Physically, we'll collect and hang on to stuff for the longest time. Go into my garage and you'll find all sorts of trinkets, gizmos, and gadgets . . . most of which have come from other trinkets, gizmos, and gadgets. How many of you have a spouse that's always asking you to pick up, clean, and, even worse, purge items from around the house? Here's how it usually goes:

Her: What about this? (Holding up something with wires sticking out of it.)

Me: I can't throw THAT out.

Her: Why not? You probably don't even know what it is.

Me: Yeah—but I want to hang on to it. It will come in handy someday.

Her: For what?

Me: I have no idea. But something. That's still some good wire.

Her: Seriously? It's just a piece of junk that's been lying around forever!

Me: Seriously. I want to keep it.

Of course, if she does succeed in getting me to throw it out, we all know what would happen. The very next week, I'll begin to fix something or work on a science project with my kids, or need a piece of wire . . . and the aforementioned piece of "junk" that would have been the perfect solution to my problem is now gone. So we keep it, not knowing why or when we will use it . . . but just knowing that someday we will.

This physical habit of collecting "just-in-case" materials is mirrored in the mental world. Our minds are constantly taking notes, whether consciously or subconsciously. Every room we enter, every conversation we have, even the colors of a sunset—all these elements get tucked away somewhere in the mental filing cabinet. It's an archive of potential inspiration waiting for the moment it can be useful.

I would say that most creative people tend to do this in their head as well as in their garages. Or maybe I should say they tend to be more conscious of doing this than the average person . . . because I would argue that we *all* do it to some extent or another, which is a good thing.

What differentiates highly creative people is how they access this mental trove. They recognize the significance of seemingly trivial memories and can pull from these archives when faced with a challenge. When you observe the world with the awareness that everything you encounter has potential value, your mental filing cabinet becomes more of an organized library than a cluttered attic.

When we walk into a room, we're all subconsciously making mental notes—the pattern in the carpet, the music playing in the background, the color combinations of the painted walls . . . a million sensory stimuli. The human memory is an amazing and complex instrument. As we're taking in the environment, our cognitive machine is instantaneously taking notes about those surroundings and filing them away without a second thought. I believe, however, that this is where those who are highly creative tend to be a little different. They understand that at any given moment we could encounter something that will be handy when it comes to Creative Cross-Pollinating. That pattern in the carpet, the music playing in the background, or those color combinations on the walls strike us in a certain way, enough to put a check mark by them before they get tucked away into our subconscious. They get added to that big pile of "dots" that we're always collecting, consciously or not.

One trick to develop this skill is to practice "mental bookmarking." If something strikes you as interesting or curious, pause for a moment and make a mental note of it. Picture a small bookmark flag in your mind, highlighting that thought or image. Later, when faced with a project or problem, you'll have a broader range of resources to pull from, enhancing your ability to creatively connect the dots.

If this isn't a skill you've developed yet, it's not too late — and it's one you should work on. Want some examples?

The Imagineer and the apple

Back in the 1960s, two of Walt Disney's original Imagineers, Art Director John Hench and one of his colleagues, Bob Gurr, were discussing lessons learned from the 1964 World's Fair and how they might be able to apply them to the new themed attractions being designed for Disneyland. One thing the Imagineers were stuck on was an efficient ride vehicle for the

Haunted Mansion. As Jason Surrell describes in his book *The Haunted Mansion: From the Magic Kingdom to the Movies*, "John happened to have a plastic apple sitting on his desk. Bob picked up the faux fruit and began to spin it completely around by the stem. Struck by the image, he remarked to John that they needed to develop a continuous chain-ride car that could rotate like the apple."[2] From this simple bit of Creative Cross-Pollination, an apple to a ride vehicle, the Haunted Mansion's iconic Doom Buggies were born.

Take a bite out of an apple, and you can see even more of a resemblance to the ride vehicles. What makes them incredibly apropos for the attraction is not only the way they swivel throughout the journey, but due to their unique shape—an apple with a bite taken out of it— guests are pointed in the exact direction they need to be, focusing their line of sight exactly where the Imagineers want it. All that from an apple.

Weeds and Velcro

According to a 2010 Time Magazine article:

> "Velcro is the brainchild of Georges de Mestral, a Swiss engineer who, in 1941, went for a walk in the woods and wondered if the burrs that clung to his trousers—and dog—could be turned into something useful. After nearly eight years of research (apparently, it's not so easy to make a synthetic burr), de Mestral successfully reproduced the natural attachment with two strips of fabric, one with thousands of tiny hooks and another with thousands of tiny loops. He named his invention Velcro, a combination

of the words velvet and crochet, and formally patented it in 1955. (It's important to note—namely, because we're legally required to do so—that Velcro is the copy-written name of a product, not a general term for the scratchy fastening system we all know and love.)"[3]

Technically, it's called a "hook-and-loop fastener," but whatever you call it, if de Mestral didn't have the ability to cross-pollinate between the weeds that clung to his pants and what ultimately became the world's first hook-and-loop fastener, you have to wonder how astronauts would keep their pens and plates from floating around in space.

Biscuits and donuts

As a Boy Scout leader, I was always looking for new and interesting recipes I could teach the boys to cook — stuff that would be easy and, most importantly, appeal to their taste. One favorite dessert that's a bit of a classic among Scouts is Dutch Oven Donuts. Creating these is super simple: you take the biscuit dough that comes in the pop-open packaging, easily found in pretty much any grocery store's refrigerated section, separate them, punch a hole in the middle, and then drop them into hot oil heated in a Dutch oven over a fire. The biscuit dough puffs up nice, fluffy, and golden brown. Scoop them out and toss them in a small paper bag filled with cinnamon sugar, and *voilà*! You have a tasty treat that kids and adults love — especially on a cool afternoon or evening when they are still warm to the touch. Cooking is full of examples of Creative Cross-Pollination, but whoever came up with the idea of turning biscuits into donuts definitely has my appreciation!

These are three very different applications of Creative Cross-Pollination, but all illustrate how people have used two seemingly unrelated bits in their mental filing cabinets—apples and ride vehicles, weeds and fasteners, biscuits and donuts—to somehow connect the dots and find a solution. Impossible for you to make those same types of links, you say? Not at all. Again, I would argue that you already do this, probably every day, and never stop to think about it. The trick, then, is to get you to think about it! Before I do that, let's take a look at some of the things that make each of us tick in terms of innate creative ability—your unique Walt Disney DNA.

A Story

This story has to do with a galaxy far, far away. We had recently completed construction of Star Tours in the (then-) Disney-MGM Studios theme park. This attraction was a highly immersive ride that took guests on a trip to the moon of Endor after boarding their Starspeeder 3000. It was a groundbreaking ride in many ways, but the engineering was most impressive, built using modified flight simulators with Audio-Animatronics synced to films displayed inside the cabin. Before guests knew what was happening, they were zipping through space to a planet far, far away. Kudos to the Imagineers who cross-pollinated technology used in the airline industry—specifically flight simulators used to train pilots—to design a wonderfully immersive attraction.

For my part, I was asked to help "plus" the exterior queue area in a small but fun way. ("Plussing" is an Imagineering term that refers to enhancements or changes made to improve an existing attraction or space.) You see, in order to begin immersing guests into the Star Tours story, Imagineers had recreated a small section of the forest of Endor, complete with massive trees that looked something like giant redwoods. You know Endor—it's that place where the Ewoks lived in *Return of the Jedi*. Anyway, one of my more interesting assignments was to write a little plaque for these trees which gave their "scientific" names and meanings. You've probably seen those little plaques in zoos or gardens with the English name, the Latin name, and a little description. Needless to say, given that these "trees" were made from concrete and steel, and I had zero training as a botanist, I knew I was going to have to get really creative with this one.

In the end, I gave the trees a proper scientific-sounding Latin name, *Sequoia pseudosom*, and explained that these trees were a species developed here on Earth from similar trees found on the Moon of Endor. They have unusually thick and hard bark (of course they do— they're made out of concrete and steel!), do not require water, and are very low maintenance (for the same aforementioned reason).

This plaque never made its way into the queue. That's not uncommon in the world of Imagineering, but it still remains one of my favorite little projects.

Summary

This chapter explores how our minds act as "filing cabinets" for experiences, observations, and ideas, which can be drawn upon later in creative endeavors. Creative individuals often accumulate mental notes or memories that, though seemingly unrelated at the time, become useful later for problem-solving. By mentally "bookmarking" interesting or curious observations, we can expand our internal library of ideas, enhancing our capacity for Creative Cross-Pollination. Developing this awareness allows for greater access to the vast mental resources we have accumulated over time.

Exercises

Try this now

Pick an object near you. Take a minute to observe and write down as many details as possible, then note any connections it brings to mind.

Try these soon

Each day, jot down one unusual observation. Reflect on any themes or recurring ideas that may connect with future tasks.

Keep a small journal and note down ideas or details you find intriguing, even if they don't have an immediate purpose. Review them weekly.

Try viewing a problem from a completely different perspective. Imagine how a child or an outsider might approach the issue and note any new insights.

Discussion Questions

1. Why is it beneficial to accumulate diverse experiences and observations, even if they don't seem immediately useful?

2. How does the concept of "mental bookmarking" relate to creativity?

3. In what ways can the contents of your "mental filing cabinet" aid in personal or professional problem-solving?

4. What habits can we develop to ensure we are mentally recording useful information?

5. How does the idea of a mental filing cabinet encourage you to explore a broader range of topics or activities?

Understanding Your

"Walt Disney DNA"

"We keep moving forward, opening up new doors
and doing new things, because we're curious.
And curiosity keeps leading us down new paths."

—Walt Disney

As a former Imagineer, I often deliver keynotes and presentations about our "Walt Disney DNA." This isn't an official concept as far as the company is concerned, but rather something that I've conceptualized and believe is pretty important to understand. Why? Because I don't think you can innovate at a high level externally without exploring what makes you tick internally. I've been extremely fortunate to work with some incredibly creative people. We were all pretty in tune with what I refer to as our Walt Disney DNA—that internal magical mix of "stuff" that allowed us to be highly innovative day in and day out. Of course it isn't just Imagineers that perform at this level, just as Navy SEALS aren't the only ones who are physically fit. But there is something internal—a self-awareness, maybe a personality disorder, as several of my friends might attest to, or perhaps zen—that helps to manifest one set of our skills at a higher level over others.

Throughout my career, and indeed my life, this Walt Disney DNA has always helped define who I am. As a college professor teaching courses in entrepreneurship, creativity, and business, I started to formally explore what made up my students' and my Walt Disney DNA—just what was the "magical mix of stuff" after all? Here's my take on it.

Understanding your creative blueprint is crucial. While everyone possesses a different set of strengths and experiences, there are common traits among those who are highly creative. These shared elements contribute to what I term your Walt Disney DNA. Recognizing and nurturing these components can significantly enhance your ability to innovate and adapt to challenges.

Since I'm using a biological analogy, I'll begin by saying that, fortunately, this Walt Disney DNA is much simpler than the DNA you learned about in biology class. Rather than containing thousands of genes, your Walt Disney DNA is comprised of five traits:

Passion

Creative people tend to have deep passion for what they do. This passion then translates into determination. If they set their mind to accomplish something that is important to them, they tend to see it through. This can take hours, weeks, days, months, or years—but eventually, the task they have been working on will get there. Sometimes this passion or determination will manifest itself spontaneously or at odd moments. That's because when a creative person is trying to innovate, the wheels in their head never stop turning. Ideas are constantly being incubated in our brains, and you never know when that "aha!" moment will come. Keep a pad and pen close by or use your smartphone to keep notes. If you think you'll remember your great idea or solution when you get home, you'll probably be disappointed—because your passionate brain is already moving on to solve other challenges laid in front of you.

Intuition

By "intuition," I am talking about what you may call a gut feeling. Having the ability to respond to this intuitive insight into the world, this "vision," is one of the hallmarks of all highly creative people. Who are some of the greatest visionaries you can think of? Plato, Dalí, Stephen Hawking, Steve Jobs, and, of course, what former Imagineer wouldn't include Walt Disney? Or it could be your own mom, dad, sister, or brother. Pick any of them and you see that they constantly have the ability to act on a hunch . . . not necessarily knowing why they know they're on the right path, but trusting in themselves and knowing they are. And, if it's yourself, you "know" what I'm describing.

Inclusiveness

Creative people have to have an open mind. They have to be inclusive and accepting of many different points of view. Being able to remain nonjudgmental throughout the innovation process is critical, because once you start dismissing ideas or shutting down other people, new approaches or potential solutions are lost before they even see the light of day. Having an open mind is one of the best ways to fill that mental filing cabinet and allows you to look at things from very different perspectives, even if that sometimes means having to go outside your comfort zone to do so. As the musician Frank Zappa once said, "A mind is like a parachute. It doesn't work if it is not open." Being unbiased, accepting, and inclusive is one of the best ways I know to power up your creative mindset.

Curiosity

Most Imagineers I know are afflicted with Peter Pan Syndrome—they don't want to grow up. Having a childlike curiosity, looking at the world from their perspective, and asking questions that only a kid would ask when you are deep within the creative process is a good thing. For some, that's not so hard. As someone who was being asked to create the magic for Disney's theme parks on a daily basis, it was not only easy but actually encouraged. For many, though, tapping into your inner child is a difficult and even awkward process. That's easy to understand, especially if you've become successful at a career that doesn't traditionally call on childlike skills. How many of you would want your attorney, CPA, corporate CEO, or police sergeant acting like a little kid? I would argue, however, that the most successful people, no matter their field, actually do act like kids . . . though they may not necessarily think about it from that perspective. However, when faced with a challenge that is difficult to solve, creative people are able to find that kid's perspective, tap into that curiosity, and make the effort to go out, learn, explore, and find answers to their questions.

Emotion

Emotional folks, us creative people are—sometimes not the easiest to deal with or be around. On the other hand, sometimes it makes us great fun to hang out with. Some creative people are driven by darker emotions, and some by pure joy. Most flip back and forth depending on what the situation or project may call for, but we're not afraid to let emotions play a part in the creative process. As a matter of fact, innovators understand that they must.

While your Walt Disney DNA can be thought of as a holistic set of traits, there are many, many individual attributes and components which affect and "program" our individual approach to innovation in an infinite number of ways. Life experiences, personalities, cultural norms, likes and dislikes, education, and, as the famous line from *Anna and the King* goes: etc., etc., etc. . . .

To some, this enormous—nay, *infinite*—combination of things that go into making up our creative being can be overwhelming if you stop to think about it and, even worse, try to analyze it. But, like most things in nature (and Creative Cross-Pollination *is* a natural process), sometimes it's best to take a more zen approach, acknowledge its existence, and just know that it "is" and that it works. On the same note, it's also important to realize that all these infinite things are intertwined within us. Remember when I said, "Creative Cross-Pollination has much to do with trusting that the 'dots' you collect throughout your life will somehow connect in the future," and "It's often amazing how they do"?

Consider this:

> A Zen master asked a young student to bring him a pail of water to cool his bath.

> The student brought the water, and after pouring most of it in to cool his master's bath, threw the remaining water over the ground.

"Think," said the master to the student. "You could have watered some of the temple's plants with those few drops you have thrown away."

The young student understood Zen at that exact moment. He changed his name to Tekisui, which means "drop of water," and lived to become a wise Zen master himself.

The moral: Sometimes, in our search for knowledge, we become so concerned with exploring the big answers (passion, responsiveness, inclusiveness, curiosity, emotion) that we forget the significance of ordinary, everyday moments—things that come naturally to us. Like the student who became careless in his routine chore, we too can forget that significance can be found in the smallest of moments, and that all of our individual experiences (like drops of water) contribute to the unique meaning of our path.

So while it is important to understand what those big answers are (think of them as the bucket), do not forget it is everything that goes into formulating those answers (the water) that contributes to your creative process. As Steve Jobs realized: *"You have to trust in something — your gut, destiny, life, karma, whatever."*

The goal is to focus on understanding what goes into making up your Walt Disney DNA and keeping yourself open to the possibilities of transformative change, which, in turn, will have profound impacts on both your professional and personal life.

Summary

"Walt Disney DNA" refers to a set of traits shared by highly creative individuals: passion, intuition, inclusiveness, curiosity, and emotional depth. These characteristics help Imagineers innovate by exploring possibilities and engaging with diverse ideas. The chapter emphasizes self-awareness, encouraging readers to understand their unique "DNA" for creativity. By nurturing and balancing these traits, individuals can access their full creative potential and approach problems with an open and curious mindset.

Exercises

Try this now

Think of a recent challenge you faced. List which Walt Disney DNA traits you applied and note any areas you might improve.

Try these soon

Reflect on a past creative project. Write down how each Walt Disney DNA trait contributed to your process.

Identify a role model who embodies the Walt Disney DNA. What can you learn from their approach to innovation?

Rank the five traits in terms of your strengths. Create a small goal to develop your lowest-ranked trait over the next month.

Discussion Questions

1. Which Walt Disney DNA traits do you identify with most, and why?

2. How does passion drive creative projects, even in the face of challenges?

3. Why is inclusiveness essential for fostering creativity and innovation?

4. How can self-awareness enhance your approach to creative problem-solving?

5. In what ways might intuition be an important guide in both personal and professional settings?

Just Who Do You Think You Are?

"When you do the common things in life in an uncommon way, you will command the attention of the world."

—George Washington Carver

Have I gotten philosophical enough for you? If not, don't worry . . . because in this section we really start to explore what makes you tick. That's important. Why? Because understanding yourself, and then drawing on that understanding to enhance your own Creative Cross-Pollination, is much like the muscle memory athletes use to perform at such high levels. Think about it. When a young quarterback is learning his pass technique, his coaches will break down every move: foot position, wrist movement, finger placement, arm follow-through, and so on. All of this information is fed to the rookie so he can adjust and hone his style. At first, much of his effort is spent thinking about all these individual components. Because of this, more than a few "ducks" are thrown as he struggles to bring it all together flawlessly and naturally. Finally, after repeating the passing motion over and over again, and with some time and patience, his throwing technique becomes second nature—he doesn't even think about it. Eventually, he finds himself at a point where whenever he takes the field, his thoughts aren't about foot position, wrist movement, finger placement, or arm follow-through anymore. It becomes about finding his open receiver and getting the ball to him in the most efficient and accurate way.

The same holds true for nurturing your creative mind. The more you engage with your creative process and practice techniques that foster innovation, the more instinctive they become. You may start by consciously thinking through each step—brainstorming, drawing connections, or deliberately stepping outside your comfort zone. But over time, these methods will start to become second nature.

So you see, Creative Cross-Pollination helps you make instinctive choices for solving challenges just as good coaching helps an athlete do the same. How many of you have been told you're "overthinking the problem" or "thinking too hard"? That's the equivalent of the quarterback focusing on his foot position or follow-through. By first breaking down some of the components which contribute to your creative side, you will understand those fundamentals which serve as the building blocks of your creative technique. Just as the coach does with their player, I'll get you thinking about them now. Then, with some time and patience, you won't be thinking about them at all—they will be part of your creative muscle memory, and you'll be throwing touchdown passes before you know it!

Self-reflection is an invaluable tool in this process. Set aside moments to ponder your strengths and the areas where you might need to grow. Are you naturally curious but hesitant to share ideas openly? Do you have strong intuition but struggle with inclusive brainstorming? Mapping out these traits can illuminate where your creative energy flows freely and where it gets stuck.

A Story

This story has to do with the time I worked on an attraction called The Great Movie Ride that used to be at the (then-) Disney-MGM Studios but sadly closed in 2017. It was a wonderful attraction, all about classic Hollywood cinema. You would get on a ride vehicle with about twenty other guests, and it would take you through recreations of scenes from some of the most famous movies ever made, like *Casablanca*, *The Wizard of Oz*, *Indiana Jones*, and even *Alien*. At one point during the ride, however, there was a big surprise. Depending on which vehicle you were in, the ride would be taken over by a classic Hollywood gangster or a bandit character straight out of the American West. In order to provide a better show for our guests, one of the things I did was write a little biography for each of those characters.

Here is the biography for the Gangster, Mugsy:

"Mugsy" is a classic prohibition-era crook, à la John Dillinger. According to police records, he is 29 years old.

His rap sheet goes back to the days when he was a kid, scamming tourists and picking pockets. Mugsy has worked his way up in the local crime scene, one bullet at a time. He is cocky and arrogant and has always felt he was one better than the next guy. Mugsy likes to exchange lead with the local authorities or, even better, with rival crooks trying to move in on his turf. Of course, sometimes he likes to move in on their turf, which has resulted in some ill feelings throughout the neighborhood.

Being a leader of the whole South Side means making sure his interests always come first. Although he is loyal to his boys, this means that everybody is expendable, particularly if it means his hide versus theirs. Mugsy has made quite a name for himself running booze to supply the local speakeasies. He normally wouldn't hurt innocent bystanders, unless he feels threatened by them. Mugsy is almost always cool and in control.

This wasn't anything the guests ever saw; it was created for the Cast Members who played those roles. This was important because it allowed everyone to understand the details of who these characters were and it helped make sure they were always portrayed the same way, resulting in a more consistent show experience.

The lesson here is that at Disney, the story is king. We do not do anything as Imagineers before having a well-thought-out story created for whatever attraction, store, theme park, restaurant, or resort we may be working on. These stories serve as the blueprint from which we create our magic. I would challenge each of you to think about creating a story whenever you are working on a project, whether big or small. What is the story you want to tell? If you can think about your work like this, it will give you a fresh perspective and help guide you from start to finish creatively, as well as give you a consistent vision—a blueprint—to work from throughout the entire project's life cycle.

Summary

This chapter delves into the importance of self-understanding in the creative process. Much like athletes develop muscle memory, creatives need to cultivate an intuitive approach to problem-solving. By identifying the core elements of one's creative personality, individuals can make creativity feel more instinctual. The chapter encourages readers to analyze and strengthen the fundamentals of their creativity to establish "creative muscle memory," allowing them to perform at a higher level naturally.

Exercises

Try this now

Take a few minutes to write down three of your creative strengths and one area for improvement.

Try these soon

Reflect on a recent project. Break down the steps you took, noting which ones felt natural and which required more thought.

Create a list of creative habits you'd like to build. Start practicing one habit regularly for the next two weeks.

Pair up with a friend or peer. Ask them to describe how they see your creative strengths and any potential areas for growth.

Discussion Questions

1. How does self-reflection contribute to developing "creative muscle memory"?

2. Why is it helpful to analyze the fundamental components of your creative process?

3. In what ways can understanding your creative personality improve your problem-solving skills?

4. How does practicing creativity regularly lead to more intuitive innovation?

5. What are some ways to identify your strengths and weaknesses in creativity?

About
Innovation

"From his neck down a man is worth a couple of dollars a day,
from his neck up he is worth anything that his brain can produce."

—Thomas Edison

We have all heard the saying, "There's no such thing as an original idea." I don't believe this. Many people lump innovation and creativity together. There is an age-old argument about this, with both sides having valid points. My view is that they are definitely separate and distinct. As I see it, you cannot be innovative without being creative — but you can certainly be creative without being innovative.

Innovation, to me, represents the tangible output of creativity when it's pushed to its fullest potential. While creativity is the conceptual process of connecting ideas in new ways, innovation is when those ideas are implemented to create something impactful. Think of creativity as the spark and innovation as the fire that warms a room or powers an entire city.

Another perspective: Today there are new technologies, processes, and other means that exist that are being used to generate some incredibly creative materials. Artificial intelligence alone has transformed the human creative process. While the new ideas generated from AI can often stand on their own, nothing can take away from the innate process of using Creative Cross-Pollination to generate something completely new.

And it's that "new" that makes innovation so thrilling. When you're on the cusp of creating something that hasn't been done before, there's an electric energy in the air. Think of Thomas Edison and the lightbulb — sure, people had used oil lamps and candles for centuries, but no one had quite turned the flicker of an idea into the steady, practical glow that could illuminate an entire room at the flick of a switch. Edison's brilliance wasn't just in his inventiveness; it was in his ability to bring all those tiny sparks of creativity together and fuse them into one groundbreaking innovation.

But here's the thing: innovation isn't always loud or monumental. It can be subtle, even quiet. It's not just building the next skyscraper or launching the latest tech product. Sometimes innovation is about finding a better way to do something that seems small yet impacts lives in meaningful ways. Take the modern zipper, for instance. It's not flashy, and it won't land you a Nobel Prize, but can you imagine life without it? What began as a series of creative attempts to improve clothing fasteners eventually led to one of the most practical everyday innovations we rely on without a second thought.

Day-to-day innovating with Creative Cross-Pollination can be even more mundane — so much so that most of the time we don't even realize we're doing it. How many of us have used a key or some other item close at hand to open a package? What about when we have something stuck between our teeth that's driving us nuts? Our dental hygienist would probably lose their mind if they saw what we used or did to remove it.

It's clear that creativity is the seed, but innovation is what makes it grow, blossom, and bear fruit. The two have a symbiotic relationship, like bees and flowers. Without creative thinking, innovation would dry up, and without the act of innovating, creative ideas would remain daydreams, relegated to the "what could have been" folder in our minds.

Think about sticky notes. The humble Post-it was born from a failed experiment—trying to find a new, stickier kind of glue. Instead, Art Fry, a 3M scientist, formulated a glue that wasn't quite sticky enough. He then used Creative Cross-Pollination and connected the dots between his not-quite-sticky-enough glue and his choir hymnbook page markers that kept falling out. The result? A seemingly simple innovation that revolutionized how we bookmark, brainstorm, and leave little "don't forget to pick up milk" reminders for our loved ones.

But innovation isn't always a solo endeavor, either. While there's a certain romantic notion of the lone genius inventing the future in their garage or lab, the reality is that many innovations are the result of collaboration. Look at the development of the smartphone. It wasn't just one person or even one company that made it happen—it was several, spawned by decades of teamwork among engineers, designers, programmers, and even dreamers who wanted to push technology forward.

So, what can we learn from this? For one, collaboration fuels innovation. If you want to take your creativity and turn it into something groundbreaking, seek out other minds to bounce your ideas off of. Whether it's a colleague, mentor, or even a friend who's known for thinking outside the box, innovation often thrives when different perspectives mix together. Remember, Creative Cross-Pollination isn't just about pulling from your own mental filing cabinet; it's about taking inspiration from the shared pool of human experience.

And speaking of shared experiences, sometimes innovation is about timing. An idea can be too far ahead of its time or emerge at just the right moment to change the game. Think about Nikola Tesla, who was undoubtedly one of the most creative minds in history. Many of his ideas were so innovative that the world wasn't ready for them—wireless electricity and advanced robotics were concepts he toyed with long before their time. Today, these once-fantastical ideas are part of ongoing technological quests that modern innovators are racing to realize.

What's crucial is to stay in that sweet spot where creativity meets practicality. This balance can be tricky to maintain. Push too far toward pure creative thinking, and you risk drifting into ideas that can't find footing in the real world. Lean too far into practicality, and you may end up rehashing what's already been done, playing it safe without pushing any boundaries.

I like to think of the innovation that comes from Creative Cross-Pollination as a dance between the left and right hemispheres of the brain. On one side, you have logic, order, and reason. On the other, imagination, intuition, and spontaneity. The most successful innovators aren't those who only rely on one side of this spectrum, but those who have learned to sway gracefully between the two, blending the rational and the inspired.

And, yes, sometimes innovation can be messy. It involves trial and error, false starts, and the occasional facepalm moment when you realize your "eureka" idea isn't as groundbreaking as you initially thought. That's okay. In fact, that's more than okay—it's necessary. Failure is an essential part of the innovative process. Each setback gives you data, shows you what doesn't work, and often leads to discoveries that you didn't even know you were looking for.

Take penicillin as a prime example. Alexander Fleming didn't set out to discover the first antibiotic. He was just cleaning up his lab and noticed that a mold had killed off bacteria in a petri dish. That small, serendipitous moment led to a medical breakthrough that has saved millions of lives. Fleming's creativity wasn't in planning to find penicillin, but in recognizing the potential of what he stumbled upon and running with it.

At the end of the day, innovation is about recognizing those little sparks of creativity, feeding them, and nurturing them until they grow into a flame that can change the world—or at least make it a bit brighter. It's about being brave enough to take your creative ideas and put them out there, even if the outcome isn't certain.

So, don't be afraid to innovate. Whether it's in your job, your hobby, or even in the way you organize your home, look for opportunities to turn your creative thoughts into action. Creative Cross-Pollination can help you do that. Remember that not every idea will change the world, and that's fine. Sometimes innovation is just about improving a small part of your day, and other times it's about adding something meaningful to someone else's life. Either way, it's worth pursuing.

Summary

Innovation is presented as the practical, impactful application of creativity. While creativity generates ideas, innovation turns them into reality. The chapter explains that innovation often involves a blend of creativity and practicality, requiring collaboration, timing, and resilience in the face of failure. It emphasizes that innovation is more than grand inventions; it can be as simple as finding a better way to complete a small task or connecting the dots born from mistakes. By using Creative Cross-Pollination as the method for solving a challenge at hand and exploring the dance between creativity and logic, readers can turn their ideas into meaningful actions.

Exercises

Try this now

Think of an everyday task you do. List one way you could improve it with a small innovation.

Try these soon

Brainstorm a list of ideas for simple improvements you could make in your environment, whether at home, work, or school.

Identify a project where you can apply innovation. Consider different perspectives on how to approach it and outline one practical change to implement.

Find a peer to discuss a current challenge. Collaborate to explore different approaches, focusing on both creative ideas and practical outcomes.

Discussion Questions

1. How does the chapter differentiate between creativity and innovation?

2. Why is it important to balance creativity with practicality in innovation?

3. In what ways can failure contribute to the innovation process?

4. Why is collaboration often essential for successful innovation?

5. How can seemingly small innovations make a significant impact?

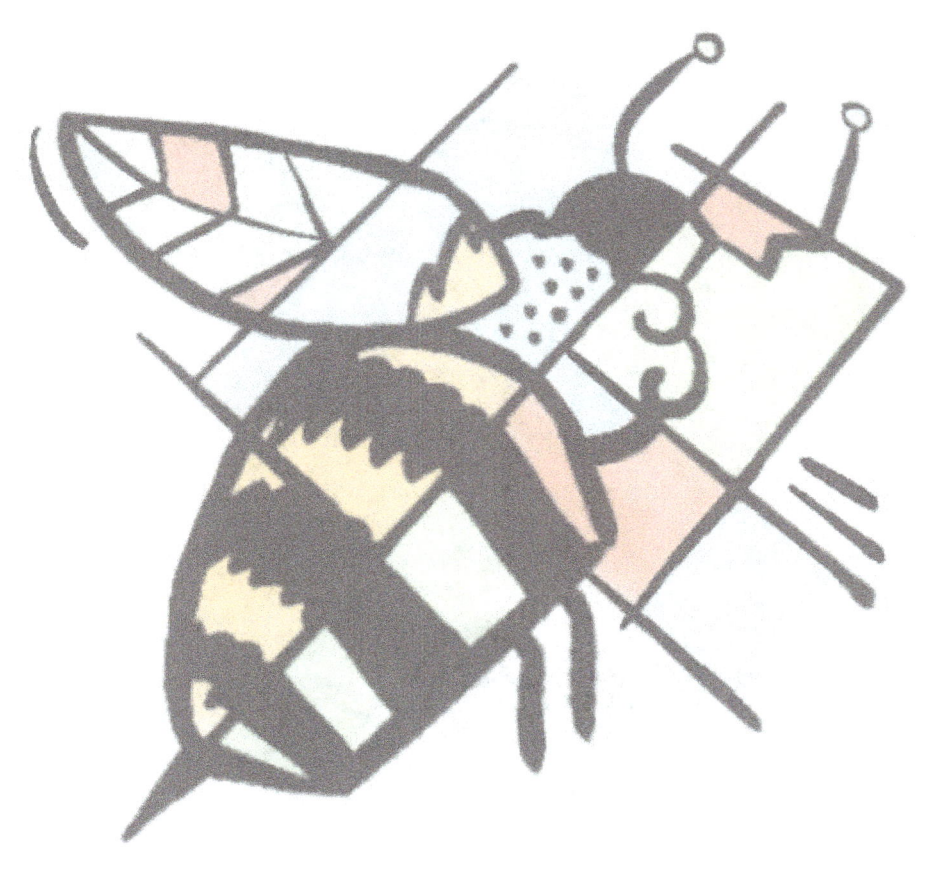

6

Soft Eyes

"Do not look at your opponent's sword, or you will be slain by his sword. Do not look into his eyes, or you will be drawn into his eyes. Do not look at him, or your spirit will be distracted."

—Morihei Ueshiba

Have you ever read any books on Eastern philosophy or business strategies? There are many out there—Sun Tzu's *The Art of War*, *The Book of Five Rings* by Miyamoto Musashi, and *The Zen Leader* by Ginny Whitelaw, to name a few. If you haven't, I recommend seeking them out. You don't need to adopt the lifestyle of a Buddhist monk or the mindset of a Shinto priest, but familiarizing yourself with these views of the world can certainly help expand your perspectives, allowing you to add more to that mental filing cabinet in ways you may not have ever considered.

One of the most powerful lessons drawn from these teachings is the concept of perception. Eastern philosophies often emphasize seeing the world not through a narrow lens but with techniques that promote an awareness that extends beyond what is directly in front of you. This approach can significantly impact how you process information, interact with your environment, and innovate.

The concept of "soft eyes" from aikido is a good example of this. Having soft eyes is one of the best ways to pay attention and a technique that can be developed by all of us. What exactly is this mysterious technique? It's hard to say exactly, but essentially it is akin to being observant of your surroundings while not focused on them. It's kind of like developing Ninja vision. If you were ever in a drum corps or the military, you may be more familiar with the close cousin of "soft eyes," peripheral vision—that way of being aware of what's to your left or your right without turning your head. It's how marching bands and marines are able to keep such straight lines while moving forward. With soft eyes, one learns to widen one's periphery, to take in more of the world.

Developing soft eyes can be transformative for problem-solving by filling in your mental filing cabinet in an almost unconscious way. Instead of honing in on a single issue or detail, you start to notice connections, patterns, and opportunities that might otherwise be overlooked. This expanded awareness fuels Creative Cross-Pollination by allowing your mind to explore more options than it would through a narrow, focused gaze.

Going a step further, take a moment to stop reading, set this book down, and stare straight ahead of you. It doesn't matter where you are, but take note of what is directly in front of you. Then, relax your vision, and start to take note of what is in your peripheral vision — to your left and right — but don't move your head or your eyes. Rather, open your perception to what is around you. Once you feel as though you've done this, take note of what is above and below the center point you are staring at, again without moving your head or your eyes. Hopefully, you're noticing that you're more aware of everything within your field of vision. It's not that you weren't seeing all this before, but now you have a heightened awareness of everything. If you can do this, then you'll experience soft eyes. If not, then practice, because it is a skill that can be learned.

Soft eyes can become a daily practice that helps you approach tasks, conversations, and challenges with a new mindset. The broader awareness it supplies can be a gateway to more holistic thinking and innovative problem-solving.

A Story

There was a young man who seemed to be highly successful in all areas of his life. He had a good job, bought a nice house, drove a nice car, and didn't seem to want for anything. Deep down, however, he felt unhappy and incomplete, though he could never quite understand why. The young man heard of a wise monk in a faraway land who, it was rumored, held the secret to living a happy and complete life. The young man, upon hearing this, sold virtually all of his earthly possessions and set off for the mountains of Asia to find this monk.

After several months of wandering from village to village, the young man finally came upon the elder for whom he was looking. "Master, I have given up everything and have traveled a long distance to learn from you. I wish to stay with you and become your disciple for as long as it might take to learn the true secret to living a fulfilling life."

"Young man," said the old monk, "I am honored you have traveled so far and sacrificed so much to learn from me. But there is no reason for you to stay for more than just a few minutes. You see, I can teach you all you need to know right now."

Confused, the young man looked at the monk. "But Master, I do not understand . . ."

The monk went on to explain: "To live a fulfilling life, there are only three things you need to know. The first thing is . . . to pay attention. The second thing is . . . to pay attention. And the third secret is . . . to pay attention."

The young man returned home having seen things he never saw before.

Summary

"Soft eyes" is a concept from aikido that encourages a wide, relaxed field of vision, allowing for greater awareness of one's surroundings. Applied to creativity, this approach allows individuals to remain open to possibilities that might be missed with a more narrow focus. The chapter suggests using this broader perspective to enhance observation skills, which can contribute to Creative Cross-Pollination by drawing insights from a wide range of sources.

Exercises

Try this now

Spend a minute relaxing your vision. Without focusing on anything specific, observe everything in your field of vision. Note any insights.

Try these soon

Practice "soft eyes" during a conversation, noticing subtle cues in the other person's body language or tone.

Choose a task and take a few minutes to observe it without judgment. List anything new you notice.

Discussion Questions

1. How can adopting a "soft eyes" perspective benefit creative problem-solving?

2. What is the value of observing your environment without focusing too closely on any one detail?

3. In what ways can broader awareness contribute to more innovative thinking?

4. How can "soft eyes" help in collaborating or brainstorming with others?

5. Why might a narrow focus sometimes limit creativity?

7

Boosting Your Chances for Innovation

"Things may come to those who wait, but
only the things left by those who hustle."

—Unknown

As I've alluded to before, being an Imagineer doesn't impart you with any sort of super creative powers, just as being a Navy SEAL doesn't impart you with superhuman strength or a college professor, incredible intellect. It's just that to reach the height of our professions, we've all learned some secrets along the way within our given fields that help us perform our jobs. With that in mind, I'd like to share some thoughts that might help you focus and tap into your creative energy.

Find your own path

"If you find a job you love, you'll never work a day in your life." This is something I wish for every student I speak to or professional who is unhappy in their job—I hope you never have to work a day in your life. How many people go through life in a career they never really had passion for? Perhaps you're one of them. This can happen for many reasons: external expectations, misplaced motivations, the fear of changing an established career, etc. Not to say that there aren't times when we need to take jobs we don't necessarily want or enjoy, but what I'm referring to here is the difference between a job and a career. In my mind, jobs are short-term employment choices that we make to reach a short-term objective, like increased income, career advancement, medical benefits, or travel. A career is something you build over your lifetime. This is where you put the focus of finding work that is truly meaningful to you—work that you enjoy. I'm certainly not suggesting that you put down this book and turn in your resignation letter tomorrow, but I am encouraging you to make a thoughtful assessment of what it is you want to do in life that will make you happy, and then plan out an effective and practical way to get there. It could take weeks, months, or years, but hopefully there is a way. Being happy and passionate about what you do is one of the greatest ways to ensure you stay creative and innovative in your work.

Believe in serendipity

I define serendipity as "unexpected good things happening." Looking down and spotting a dollar bill on the ground. Getting an extra bagel tossed in with your order. Walking into a room, locking eyes with someone, and finding a partner to spend the rest of your life with. It happens. Serendipitous moments occur in life and in work. As Steve Jobs noted, you may call it "luck," "karma," or "fate," but however you refer to it, I think it's important to believe that these moments occur and not only appreciate them but know and take comfort that even in your toughest times they will occur. If and when they do, I would challenge you to see if perhaps there is a way to capitalize on your good fortune.

Trust your inner "voices"

Hearing voices? You're not nuts. We all do, and that's okay (unless they're the kind of voices that people hear in horror movies). For the most part, these voices we hear go back to one of the five components I wrote about earlier: intuition. Recognizing that these inner voices actually exist goes back hundreds of years, probably more. Plato, the Athenian philosopher who lived during the Classical period in Ancient Greece some 2,400 years ago, described three ways of "knowing" things: the physical world, reason, and "divine madness." The physical way was learning through our basic physical senses: sight, sound, touch, hearing, and smell. Reason is the cognitive way of learning, through education, debate, study, etc. Then there was this concept of divine madness. What Plato was referring to here is knowing something is right, but not really knowing why we know that. Intuition equates with Plato's divine madness—responding to those gut feelings you may occasionally have. The key here is to sometimes stop and listen to what those internal voices are saying, positive or negative, and perhaps surrender to wherever they come from. You may just find out you've given yourself some of the best advice you could get.

Embrace the unknown

Innovation often requires taking risks and stepping into areas where you might not feel entirely comfortable. Whether that means exploring a new industry, learning a new skill, or brainstorming with people outside your usual circle, embracing the unknown can yield unexpected and exciting results.

Develop a bit of swagger (but not too much)

There is nothing wrong with knowing you are good at what you do and that you have sharp instincts. Whatever you call it — responsiveness, divine madness, a gut feeling, or anything else — what's important here is to believe and trust in yourself. Why is this important? Well, let's stop to make a list of some of the highest achievers in any field or walk of life: Abraham Lincoln, Oprah Winfrey, Napoleon, Michelangelo, Bill Gates, and, dare I say, Walt Disney. Obviously, the list can go on and on — and not just with famous people. Think about a former teacher, a colleague, your mom or dad, and of course, our distant cousin Ug. One thing these high achievers all have in common is an almost divine-like self-confidence. They believe in themselves. Sometimes that self-confidence manifests itself as arrogance, and that's obviously not a good thing. However, if tempered in a healthy way, I like to think of it more as "swagger."

Learn how to play with others—and speak their language

I'm convinced there are basically two types of people when it comes to communication styles. There are some folks (which I will refer to as Type 1) who, if you ask how their day is going, will answer with an abrupt "Fine" . . . and that's it! Then there are people like me, Type 2 — if you ask the same question, you'll not only hear how my day is going but also how my week is going, how my dog's week is going, how last week went, and what I'm doing next week. Now the interesting thing is that Type 1s and Type 2s often misinterpret the other's communication styles. Because Type 2s are very extroverted, they often wonder what they did to offend a Type 1 or why that person is upset with them. Type 1s, on the other hand, may be thinking, "Why doesn't this person shut up?" and, "Can't they just give me a concise, clear answer?" Sound familiar? If you understand that different people communicate in different ways, it will be much easier to have conversations by knowing how to adapt appropriately. So much of creativity and innovation relies on working with others and on teams — it can't always just be about you. The better you can communicate with your team, the easier things will be.

Maintain a growth mindset

Challenges are opportunities to learn and grow, not roadblocks. People with a growth mindset don't shy away from difficulties; they dive into them, knowing that every failure is a step closer to success.

Understand the Corridor Principle

The Corridor Principle states that with every venture launched, new and unintended opportunities often arise. Think of it this way: Embarking on any given venture (or life itself) is like walking down a long corridor with plenty of doors on both sides. At any time, one of these doors can open up, providing a new pathway to travel down. At that point you can make the decision to keep moving ahead, heading down the new "hallway," or perhaps explore this new pathway, seeing what's there and making a note to come back and explore more after heading further down your original corridor.

Earlier I wrote about how creativity is often heuristic rather than algorithmic. I also wrote about the importance of having an open mind and believing in serendipity. One of the reasons why all of these things are so important is the Corridor Principle. Innovation and Creative Cross-Pollination take a degree of flexibility. Because you are trying to build something unique and new, it's very possible that things aren't going to progress as you expect them to, for better or worse. As a matter of fact, often these unexpected results will lead you in a completely new direction. That's not necessarily a bad thing, as many discoveries were made by accident and came to be because people recognized the Corridor Principle at work.

A Story

Post-it notes are a classic example of the Corridor Principle. The invention unfolded like this:

If you were to ask someone at 3M in the late 1960s what their next big breakthrough would be, chances are they wouldn't have guessed "sticky notes." After all, this was a company known for serious, industrial-grade adhesives — the kind that held together aircraft parts, not flimsy little squares of yellow paper. But fate, as it often does, had other plans.

The first accident that set everything in motion happened in 1968, when a chemist named Spencer Silver was trying to develop a super-strong adhesive for the aerospace industry — something that would bond with unwavering strength. Instead, he stumbled upon something completely unexpected: a weak, pressure-sensitive adhesive made of Acrylate Copolymer Microspheres. Unlike traditional adhesives, this one had a peculiar quirk — it could stick to surfaces but peel off effortlessly without leaving any residue behind. And even more intriguingly, it was reusable. You could slap it onto something, peel it off, and stick it again without losing its effectiveness.

Silver knew he had discovered something interesting, but the problem was nobody else at 3M saw the value in an adhesive that wasn't particularly sticky. He spent five years pitching it internally, hoping someone would see its potential. But time and time again, he was met with polite nods and indifferent shrugs. No one — not even Silver himself—could come up with a truly marketable use for it. It was shelved, seemingly destined to be another one of those cool-but-useless scientific discoveries.

Enter Geoff Nicholson, who became the product's laboratory manager at 3M in 1973. Silver wasted no time approaching him with samples, hoping that maybe—just maybe—Nicholson would see something that others had missed. At the time, the best idea Silver had was to use the adhesive for a new kind of bulletin board—one where you could stick paper to it without push pins or tape and then remove it without damaging the paper. A neat concept, sure, but not exactly a business revolution. Bulletin boards weren't exactly flying off the shelves.

Then came the second accident, and this one changed everything.

A chemical engineer at 3M, Art Fry, had attended one of Silver's seminars about this odd adhesive, but he didn't think much of it at the time. Outside of work, Fry sang in a church choir in St. Paul, Minnesota. He had a small but irritating problem—his bookmarks kept falling out of his hymnal during services. One day, in a moment of brilliance, he thought, "What if I put Silver's adhesive on the back of my bookmarks? That way, they'd stay put but wouldn't damage the pages."

Eureka.

He rushed back to Nicholson and Silver, practically buzzing with excitement. They had been thinking about the adhesive all wrong! Instead of putting it on a bulletin board, why not put it on paper? That way, you could stick it to anything! The idea seemed so simple, so obvious in hindsight, yet no one had thought of it before.

Of course, turning the idea into a real product wasn't as easy as slapping some glue onto paper. Early prototypes had a frustrating flaw: the adhesive would sometimes detach from the paper and remain on the surface it was stuck to, or worse, leave behind a messy residue. This wasn't going to work. So, two other 3M employees, Roger Merrill and Henry Courtney, were brought in to develop a special coating that would keep the adhesive bonded to the paper without transferring. After much trial and error, they succeeded.

And yet, even with a working product in hand, 3M's management still wasn't convinced. They shelved it for another three years. Even though employees at 3M were using and loving the sticky notes in their own offices, executives didn't believe there was a real market for them. Finally, in 1977, they gave it a shot and launched test sales of what they called "Press 'n Peel" notes in a few cities.

And it bombed.

The problem wasn't the product—it was the marketing. No one understood why they needed it. 3M executives were ready to pull the plug for good, but Nicholson and his boss, Joe Ramey, refused to let it die. They had a gut feeling that if people just tried the product, they'd fall in love with it. So, they came up with a radical new plan.

In 1978, they launched what they called "The Boise Blitz." Instead of advertising, they flooded Boise, Idaho, with free samples. Businesses, secretaries, and office workers all received stacks of these strange little sticky notes. And this time something magical happened— people got it. They used them, they loved them, and most importantly, they wanted more. When 3M checked back, an astonishing 90% of the people who had received free samples placed reorders. To put that into perspective, this was twice the success rate of any product 3M had ever launched.

Two years later, in 1980, Post-it notes were officially released nationwide. What had once been seen as a useless mistake became one of the most beloved office supplies in history. Today, Post-it notes are among the top five best-selling office products in the world.

All because of a failed adhesive, a lost hymnal bookmark, and a good deal of Creative Cross-Pollination!

Bonus fact: Ever wonder why the standard color for Post-it notes is yellow? It turns out this was kind of an accident as well. The official story from some at 3M is that it was because it created a "good emotional connection with users" and that it would "contrast well stuck to white paper." However, according to Geoff Nicholson there was no such thought given to the color. The real reason Post-it notes were yellow was simply because the lab next door to where they were working on the Post-it note "had some scrap yellow paper—that's why they were yellow, and when we went back and said, 'Hey guys, you got any more scrap yellow paper?' they said, 'You want any more, go buy it yourself,' and that's what we did, and that's why they were yellow."

To me it was another one of those incredible accidents. It was not thought-out; nobody said they'd better be yellow rather than white because they would blend in. It was a pure accident and, as mentioned earlier, a classic example of the Corridor Principle in action. Other classic "happy accidents" and examples of Creative Cross-Pollination that emerged from various labs and initiatives include microwave ovens, aspartame (NutraSweet®), ScotchGard® fabric protector, Teflon®, and X-rays.

Here's another example, although this one isn't a happy accident. It illustrates how I used Creative Cross-Pollination intentionally.

A Story

As Imagineers we try to engage as many senses as we
can to tell our stories and immerse our guests into the
perfect environment. Lighting, audio, smells, projections
. . . it's all fair game in an Imagineer's toolkit. A few years
ago, this approach to immersion served me well when I
was asked to help an instructor, Daniel McComb, who
at the time worked with young adults with special needs
at Cardinal Newman College in Preston, England. He is
a big Disney fan and asked if I could perhaps give him
some ideas for a sensory room he wanted to create for
the students to use if they were having a tough day. It's
designed to be a safe place used for relaxation, parent
meetings when students have their annual reviews,
student counseling sessions throughout the week, and
other similar needs. All of these situations can cause
anxiety, so anything to lessen that is much needed.

Daniel, who is very talented and artistic, started the
room on his own by injecting some artwork and props
that he created based on the Pixar movie *Inside Out*. He
eventually reached out to me to collaborate. Daniel was
particularly interested to see if there were ways he could
inject some "Imagineering magic" into the room on a
shoestring budget. It turned out to be an unexpected
labor of love.

It began in earnest with a video call, where I started
by giving him some ideas of how we could tap into the
different senses described earlier, using scents, lighting,
audio . . . all those things we use to tell the stories in the
parks. Daniel and I then met up and did a walk-through

of the Magic Kingdom during a planned trip to the United States shortly after we started talking. I showed him a bunch of examples related to all the things we had spoken about; he took these Imagineering techniques and did an amazing job with his talents crafting the room. We also emailed back and forth quite a bit. Talk about Creative Cross-Pollination!

Some of the things we Imagineered were: using color lights or black light to create a cool, different type of magical environment (as seen in many of Disney's classic dark rides), injecting different scents into the room (as Imagineers have been known to do within attractions or other guest areas), having different music and sounds available for atmosphere (effectively used throughout the parks to set a mood or enhance an environment), giving the students disposable 3D glasses (an effect that really pops under the black light!), adding different tactile stimulations (similar to what might be used within a ride's queue), and even simple projection mapping (most dramatically seen on the exterior of Cinderella Castle during the nighttime fireworks shows). Each of these techniques key off of various senses that students might positively respond to, depending on their preferences.

You might be wondering what ideas we came up with to execute all this. Cardinal Newman College certainly does not have the budget or resources that Walt Disney World does. Here, then, are some of my suggestions that Daniel implemented to transform the sensory room into a truly unique and magical environment. For lighting effects, standard light was replaced with color or black light; LED strips also worked nicely. Air fresheners, available in a variety of scents, simply plugged into the walls and infused the room with wonderful smells. A small Bluetooth player stored music and environmental sounds found in nature. Dimensional props and accents were installed, such as covering a column in the center of the room to look like a tree. Even some simple projection-mapping effects were created by using an inexpensive miniature LED projector. Many of these elements can easily be controlled by Daniel to fit students' preferences with a remote control that triggers everything—the audio, lights, scents, etc.

It's been a terrific project and one that we are continuing to evolve. Needless to say, the administration, parents, instructors, and especially the students have all responded in an incredibly positive way. Cross-pollinating Imagineering techniques in this way and for these students has been one of the most gratifying projects of my career.

Summary

This chapter shares additional insights and practical tips for enhancing creativity and innovation, emphasizing self-confidence, flexibility, and the importance of following your interests. It encourages readers to remain open to unexpected opportunities and to develop a sense of "swagger" in their abilities. By embracing serendipity and understanding one's communication style, readers can enhance collaboration and take advantage of unplanned pathways that arise.

Exercises

Try this now

Reflect on a recent situation where you had to adapt quickly. Note what helped you remain flexible and any takeaways for future challenges.

Try these soon

List three areas where you can develop self-confidence in your creative abilities. Create a small goal for each area.

Seek out one unexpected opportunity this week — try an unfamiliar activity or have a conversation with someone new.

The next time you work in a group, observe each person's communication style and how you might adapt to make collaboration smoother.

Discussion Questions

1. How can self-confidence impact one's ability to innovate?

2. Why is flexibility important in the creative process?

3. In what ways can serendipity play a role in innovation?

4. How might understanding communication styles aid in creative teamwork?

5. How does the chapter suggest balancing confidence with humility?

8

Reliquiae Mentis

"A creative life is an amplified life. It's a bigger life, a happier life, an expanded life, and a hell of a lot more interesting life."

—Elizabeth Gilbert

For those of you not proficient in Latin, *Reliquiae Mentis* translates to "the Remains of the Mind," which I thought would be a fitting title for my last formal chapter as I offer up some final thoughts. By now, you've seen how Creative Cross-Pollination has shaped inventions, art, and even the simplest of daily improvements. Now the question is: How will you use it tomorrow? My hope is that you will now be more cognizant of not only what CCP is but the fact that you do it many times a day. Knowing this, you will be able to consciously tap into Creative Cross-Pollination at your behest, whether in work, hobbies, or relationships. In other words, you're stepping onto a path and joining the colony of other cross-pollinators, dreamers, and boundary-breakers around the world!

The bees knew first

When I first introduced this concept, I leaned on the bees. They've been at this whole cross-pollination game far longer than humans. Nature designed them to take pollen from one flower and deposit it into another, creating something stronger, more resilient, and more alive than either flower could have achieved on its own. That's the simplest metaphor for Creative Cross-Pollination—taking something from over here, mixing it with something over there, and ending up with something delightfully unexpected.

Our prehistoric friend Ug figured it out when he smeared berry juice on the walls of his cave to make art. Leonardo da Vinci saw it in bird wings as he imagined flying machines. The Wright brothers caught it again as they watched seagulls and sketched their way into history. And you? You've done it when you improvised a tool out of a paperclip, connected an idea from your hobby to a challenge at work, or borrowed a trick from another field and surprised yourself with how well it worked. Bees, berries, and breakthroughs—different dots on the same canvas.

Your mental filing cabinet

One of my favorite analogies is the "mental filing cabinet." Creative folks—and really, all of us—are collectors. We tuck away sights, sounds, feelings, even snippets of conversations in the back of our minds. It's not junk; it's raw material. Like the Imagineer who spun a plastic apple and realized it could inspire a rotating ride vehicle for the Haunted Mansion. Or Georges de Mestral, who came home from a walk with burrs on his socks and thought, huh, these little hooks are onto something—hello, Velcro.

Everyday life gives us these deposits, and cross-pollinators are simply better at withdrawing them when the time is right. The trick is to practice noticing. Bookmark the unusual, the oddly shaped, the funny color combination, the way the air smells before a storm. You don't need to know what you'll do with it. Just trust that one day those dots will connect.

Discovering your "Walt Disney DNA"

As I reflected on my Imagineering days, I started thinking about what made some people endlessly creative. It wasn't that we had secret Imagineer pixie dust (though that would be nice). It was that we shared a certain DNA. I call it the "Walt Disney DNA," and it boils down to five traits:

Passion: that relentless drive to see something through, even if it takes years.

Intuition: trusting your gut when the map hasn't been drawn yet.

Inclusiveness: keeping your parachute-mind open, welcoming ideas no matter where they come from.

Curiosity: channeling your inner Peter Pan and asking questions only a child would dare ask.

Emotion: leaning into the highs and lows, letting feelings power your work rather than stifle it.

These aren't mystical powers. They're everyday traits we can nurture. Recognizing them in yourself is like looking at your own creative DNA strand and realizing, "Oh, so that's why I'm wired this way." Once you see it, you can lean on it.

Knowing yourself: creative muscle memory

Another layer to this is self-awareness. Athletes train until their movements become automatic. Quarterbacks don't think about wrist angles once they've thrown ten thousand passes. In the same way, creatives build muscle memory. At first, you might be deliberate: "Okay, I'll brainstorm five weird options, then I'll step back and look for connections." Over time, though, it becomes second nature.

That's why reflecting on who you are — what sparks you, what slows you down — matters. When I wrote background bios for cast members playing gangsters on The Great Movie Ride, it wasn't just flavor text. It was a framework that made their performance more authentic. Knowing the story, even if the audience never saw it, gave them confidence and consistency. Knowing yourself does the same.

Creativity vs. innovation

We've all heard the cynical line: "There's no such thing as an original idea." I don't buy it. Creativity and innovation may be siblings, but they're not identical twins. Creativity is the spark — connecting dots in new ways. Innovation is what happens when you take that spark and build a campfire with it.

Think of Post-its. A weak glue and a frustrated choir singer collided, and suddenly the world had sticky notes. Or think of penicillin — Alexander Fleming wasn't trying to cure infections that day, but he noticed mold doing something unusual and had the presence of mind to run with it. Sometimes innovation is monumental; other times it's a better zipper, a rotated ride vehicle, or simply a fork used to open a package because you don't have scissors handy.

The dance between creativity and innovation is equal parts messy and magical. Failures? They're not only inevitable but necessary. Each flop is just another dot waiting to connect.

Soft eyes: seeing more by focusing less

One of the more subtle lessons in the book came from aikido: soft eyes. Instead of staring hard at the problem in front of you, soften your gaze. Expand your awareness. Notice what's in the periphery. That's when you start to see connections that a narrow focus misses.

It's a bit like hiking in the woods. If you only look at your boots, you'll miss the eagle overhead, the mushrooms at the base of the tree, or the way the light bends through the leaves. In creativity, "soft eyes" means noticing the hints, the side trails, the happy accidents. It's about paying attention — not just to what's obvious, but to everything swirling around the edges.

Boosting your chances for innovation

By now, you've probably realized that Creative Cross-Pollination isn't about waiting for lightning to strike; you can increase your odds. Here are a few ways:

Find your own path. Work at something that actually lights you up. Otherwise, you're forcing sparks in a rainstorm.

Believe in serendipity. **Those unexpected good things? They're out there. The key is to notice and capitalize on them.**

Trust your inner voice. **Plato called it "divine madness." You might call it intuition. Either way, don't ignore it.**

Embrace the unknown. **Growth comes from leaning into discomfort, not tiptoeing around it.**

Develop some swagger. **Confidence fuels risk-taking, but temper it so it doesn't tip into arrogance.**

Learn to play with others. **Cross-pollination thrives on collaboration. Recognize different communication styles and meet people where they are.**

Keep a growth mindset. **Failures are steps, not walls.**

Understand the Corridor Principle. **Every venture opens unexpected doors. Peek through them. Some will change your trajectory entirely.**

The 3M Post-it saga is a perfect example of the Corridor Principle. An adhesive that wasn't sticky enough turned into a product used in offices, classrooms, and refrigerators worldwide. All because someone recognized a side door worth opening.

Stories that stick

Throughout the book, I've sprinkled stories—from Imagineering days, from history, from Scouts cooking donuts over campfires. They aren't just anecdotes; they're proof that Creative Cross-Pollination is everywhere.

- A plastic apple became the inspiration for the Haunted Mansion's Doom Buggies.

- Burrs on a sock turned into Velcro.

- Biscuit dough became donuts.

- Airline flight simulators turned into Star Tours.

These stories remind us that innovation isn't about conjuring something from thin air. It's about being awake enough to see the possibilities already around you.

Why this matters

So why harp on all of this? Because the world is in constant need of problem-solvers, dreamers, and tinkerers who don't just accept the obvious. Whether you're a surgeon looking for a new technique, a teacher trying to reach students in fresh ways, or simply a parent figuring out how to keep dinner interesting, Creative Cross-Pollination is your ally.

It democratizes creativity. You don't need to be a "creative professional" to use it. You just need to be willing to notice, connect, and experiment. In fact, the more diverse the group of pollinators, the more resilient and vibrant the hive becomes.

Your turn

If there's a single thread running through this book, it's this: Creative Cross-Pollination is not a trick reserved for a few. It's hardwired into us, as natural as bees buzzing between flowers. The question is whether we'll wake up to it, nurture it, and wield it intentionally.

When you do, the results ripple. A better idea at work. A more engaging class. A hobby project that unexpectedly becomes a business. A relationship enriched because you tried a different perspective. Each act of cross-pollination strengthens the ecosystem we all share.

Closing thoughts

As I wrap this up, I keep thinking back to the phrase "The Remains of the Mind." What remains after all these stories, exercises, and reflections? Hopefully, a sense that creativity is not a rare gift but a renewable practice. That your quirks, curiosities, and even your stumbles are part of a larger pattern waiting to connect. That you're part of a living colony of cross-pollinators who, in their own small ways, are nudging the world forward.

And remember—throughout this book, I've sprinkled exercises designed to get you practicing. They're not homework. They're invitations. Play with them. Twist them. Invent your own. Because the more you do Creative Cross-Pollination, the more natural it becomes.

So, as a final send-off, I'll leave you with this: I've given you several exercises already, but here are some more to have fun with . . .

1. Write down an idea for a tool, product, or service that combines two things from your world that normally don't go together. Don't worry if it's absurd—Velcro was inspired by weeds, after all. For example: "a coffee mug that also works as a Wi-Fi hot spot."

   My crazy idea:

2. Imagine a newspaper headline from ten years in the future touting the amazing benefits of something you created through cross-pollination. Write the headline here.

   My headline:

   Now write down what dots you connected to create your invention.

   The dots:

3. Creative Cross-Pollination Bingo

Check off the following as you complete them.
Once you get BINGO, reward yourself!

Bizz-Buzz Bingo

**When you can cross off all the techniques
below, you will be a master cross-pollinator!**

Asked "What would [famous figure/role model in another field] do?"

Imagined how a different industry would solve your challenge.

Took a break (walk, stretch, meditation) that sparked a new connection.

Read an article or book or watched a video outside your usual area of interest.

Connected two ideas that didn't seem related.

Wondered "How would a Disney Imagineer approach this?"

Used humor to unlock a new idea.

Walked away from your challenge for at least 24 hours to let ideas incubate.

Found inspiration in music, art, or performance to solve your challenge.

9

Creative
Cross-Pollination
in Action

"Nothing is a waste of time if you use the experience wisely."

—Auguste Rodin

THE COUNSELOR

Shivangi Maniar
Gurgaon, Haryana, India

Shivangi is an emotions coach, couples therapist, movement therapist, and cofounder of OTLO, a family-centric platform that recreates lines of communication between children, teens, and parents so that families become a cohesive unit.

As a trainer for children and teens, I have noticed that Creative Cross-Pollination is at the core of coaching. Building a solid, authentic curriculum for a workshop requires a certain synthesis—a waltz with the neurons around the brain, if you will!

What works for me?

Meditation

Over the years, meditation has helped tremendously. At first, it was my to-do lists that would float in front of my eyes; now, if I am lucky, ideas bubble up to the surface, to the extent that I often need to scramble around for a pencil before the thought slips out of mind. My bedside diary is a big muddled warehouse of letters and numbers!

To this end, I believe, CCP is accessing a band of higher, deeper knowledge, available to all. You might often think that you picked up cog A and fit it into machine B to achieve an inner "yes!" But it seems that the cloud carries the resources for you to choose from and fill the gap you face.

Thus, CCP essentially involves clearing the cobwebs of your active mind and leveraging your dormant mind to fish out creative solutions, so that the world has no option but to stand up and applaud when you present your ideas!

Intention

Intention is primary.

To the unknown, I have been a blogger for the past decade. Initially, my blogs were a collection of my experiences and insights as a mother as well as a trainer. All three—my childhood, motherhood, and work—were sufficient to dole out a two-hundred-word blog every day.

With time, though, I realized that I was running out of fodder.

To bridge the gap, my focus shifted from "I" to the world and its miniscule bits. Since then, the thought sphere has expanded, and now, every conversation, incident, or story is read and listened to with a certain level of concentration—for I do not know when I can map it to a message that I have for the world.

Thus, a pure, solid intention has the capacity to bring a thought or idea to the forefront, just loud enough for you to sit up and take notice!

To close, I truly believe that every interaction or event is a message of sorts, a communication from the Universe, and hence, must be well-received in full faith for it to manifest into a creative outlet.

THE EDUCATOR

Martin Rayala, PhD
Los Angeles, California, USA

Martin is a thought leader in education, schooling, and lifelong learning, supporting educational transformation across the world. He is also the founder of the Ensō Education Institute.

Cross-pollination has become a metaphor for the idea that something from one area can spark innovation in another area. The architect Frank Lloyd Wright looked at the low, horizontal buildings in Japan and created a style of architecture called the Prairie Style, that was more sensitive to the contours, colors, shapes and materials of the local environment. Walt Disney took ideas he developed for making animated films and added the art and craft of storytelling to traditional roadside carnivals to create a new form of amusement parks called theme parks.

The field of education struggles with the tendency of some people to create silos that inhibit such cross-pollination. Decades of attempts at developing multidisciplinary, interdisciplinary, and transdisciplinary learning have found it hard to overcome the tendency for some people to isolate themselves in the specialties with which they are most comfortable and experienced.

When we created an innovative high school that won a $10 million XQ Super School award to transform education, we found that, despite our best efforts, it was difficult to break out of the traditional standardized education model of courses and Carnegie units with fixed scope and sequences. We found it hard to change the school day and school calendar if it didn't match up with family vacations and the bus schedules of siblings at other schools. We found that some teachers had been trained to be good at their specialties and compete rather than collaborate with other subject areas for students, spaces, and resources. Some students were confused and suspicious when asked to create their own projects based on their personal interests and abilities. Some administrators didn't know how to guide or evaluate teachers who didn't seem to be "teaching" or managing classrooms in the ways they expected. Some families were looking for the standard markers of student success they had become accustomed to seeing. Some universities were just learning to seek measures of student success other than course transcripts and scores on high-stakes standardized tests to help make student admissions decisions. Some local, state, and national standards and regulations had created course names, numbers, and content expectations that locked learning into specific courses and years.

Ensō Education Institute is developing alternatives to standardized curriculum, instruction, and assessment to meet the needs of twenty-first-century learning by cross-pollinating with successful new ideas from businesses, theme parks, video games, virtual reality, architecture, entertainment, media, and design. We are rethinking why, what, where, when, and how people learn. Not all education needs to take place in schools and classrooms. Not all students need to be on the same page at the same time. Not all student achievement can be measured by a standardized test. Education can make better use of storytelling to engage learners by drawing ideas from theme parks, gamification, and virtual reality.

Think about how to use cross-pollination to design new possibilities for education.

- What if some "big-box schools" learned from Amazon that you don't need big-box stores for people to make purchases? Can we decentralize learning?

- What if some teachers had more control over where and when they teach the way Uber and Lyft drivers do? Can we create more flexibility and personal control in teachers' careers?

- What if some "classrooms" could be found in museums, zoos, environmental centers, businesses, theaters, parks, and any number of spaces? Can we develop more "real-world" learning environments?

- What if we understood that Google reduces the need for some memorization and rote learning and frees up time for more productive education?

- What if some students could learn anything, anywhere, anytime they needed to? Can we develop learning that is more personalized and responsive to learners' needs?

- How is it possible that a field whose purview includes all the most exciting adventures in history, the most amazing discoveries in science, as well as the most moving and reflective stories in the arts and humanities, somehow made it boring and unmotivating for some students? What would it take to make schools the happiest places on the planet?

Transforming education, schooling, and learning is the grand global design challenge Ensō Education Institute has taken on during the Decade of Imagination 2020–2030, and we have already made some promising advances in places as diverse as the great outdoors of the Upper Midwest, the jungles and savannas of East Africa, and the urban metropolises of New York and Los Angeles. We are living in the most exciting and productive time in the history of humanity. There will be greater changes in the next twenty years than in the entire history of the world. This is the Decade of Imagination.

If you are a thought leader in education or just want to help make the world a better place, we invite you to begin your own "hero's journey" and become part of the Ensō Circle of like-minded pathfinders at www.ensoeducation.com.

THE IMAGINEER

Theron Skees
Orlando, Florida, USA

Theron is a former senior creative executive at Walt Disney Imagineering, where he led multi-billion-dollar projects worldwide, aligning story, strategy, and experience design to create results that endure. Now, as founder of The Designer's Creative Studio, Theron shares his expertise through consulting, keynote speaking, and his book, Creating Memorable Worlds.

As an Imagineer, I've seen cross-pollination take many forms. Two examples that come to mind are the reimagining we did when creating a world-class cruising experience and my work at Hong Kong Disneyland.

For my five years leading creative at the Disney Cruise Line, my teams collaborated to develop brand-new design and experience ideas for the guest cabins in the company's three new ships. The variety of subject matter experts on this effort was very diverse on this project, which usually produces the best results. Some came from the cruise industry, some from a more traditional hotel background, and then there were experience design folks like me who really didn't come from those worlds at all! That was an intentional choice, though. Walt believed that, when trying to reach a creative solution, bringing people together who thought "differently" always generated the best range of ideas and solutions . . . and he had a particular knack for it. If you study the history of the Haunted Mansion attraction design, you'll see how two very different styles in Rolly Crump and Marc Davis came together to create a classic attraction. I believe in this approach as well and have often used the same technique in my ideation work. In this case, it worked out very nicely.

By the time our teams finished with the creative development phase, we had come up with many innovations, not just for Disney Cruise Line but the whole cruise industry—everything from reconfigurable furniture to ways of expanding the size of their cabins. In addition, we created some very unique Disney storytelling that differentiates the new ship's guest cabins and decks from the existing fleet. Most of these ideas came from cross-pollinating ideas from three multiple and distinct points of view, really listening to every participant, then combining them to create something very different but magical!

Hong Kong Disneyland involved a different type of Creative Cross-Pollination altogether. There, one of my team's major challenges was how to tell stories that would resonate not only in the Disney style but also appeal to primarily Asian audiences, many of them for their very first time. Remember, when Hong Kong Disneyland opened, it represented the first time a Chinese audience had visited a Disney park and enjoyed Disney storytelling in a physical place. One of the main challenges we had to overcome was the unfamiliarity of how to experience a Disney attraction. We discovered that it was very important to begin telling the "story" of the attraction in more detail much earlier in the process. This began by offering a clear indication of what was inside the buildings, as Asian visitors were less likely to go inside if they did not know what to expect. By borrowing some of the techniques that we, as Imagineers, traditionally use to begin unfolding the story once inside and adapting them to the outside, we were able to enhance and, in some ways, redefine the way we had been designing attractions . . . from the inside out! In the theme park expansions that have taken place in Hong Kong Disneyland, visitors can now see this technique in the Grizzly Gulch and Toy Story lands. This discovery and adaptation of attraction storytelling would not have been possible without a cross-pollination of not just ideas and designs but cultural insights as well.

THE MARKETING/COMMUNICATIONS PROFESSIONAL

Amanda Fleising, MBA
Montreal, Quebec, Canada

Amanda has built her career specializing in the B2B SaaS space, with a focus on building out and leading marketing teams, including vendor agencies, to drive pipeline and revenue. She is also an experienced entrepreneur and founder.

From the mental library of ideas many marketers or creatives store for future reference to the need to always have a notebook (or phone!) to save those sparks of creativity that are gone in a flash—all of this and more is covered in Brian's wonderfully detailed and actionable new book, *Creative Cross-Pollination*. I was able to recognize some of my traits and pick up guidance to improve my own processes. This book is a must-read for anyone looking to harness and develop the creativity we all have inside. All types of readers will benefit from the concepts here: those seeking a new career path, wanting to formalize their creative process, or looking to add creativity and bring new ideas to their current circumstances.

Marketing minds are usually on the more creative side of the spectrum when compared to many of their general business peers. Perhaps this is why, as a ballroom dancer, I always felt drawn to the marketing and advertising sides of the corporate world.

For the last twenty years, I've had very different passions that led me down separate yet somehow parallel paths: ballroom dancing and business. I grew up around entrepreneurship. My father started his company before I was born, and by the time I was old enough, I would help with marketing mailers or replace the receptionist during winter or summer breaks. I applied myself to the fullest and enjoyed learning from others. Between negotiating, assessing the cost of projects, filing invoices, and finally getting to do a full two-year rotation between all departments, there were always lessons to be learned.

I started ballroom dancing around the same time as I started working at the family business. I had always been active with different sports and was already an avid equestrian, but something about ballroom dancing, particularly Latin American styles, really drew me in. Learning my first few steps and then jumping into various types of dances was just the start. Very quickly I began spending most of my free time at the dance studio, particularly when horseback riding became quite the challenge after my horse faced several back-to-back injuries.

Long story short, I kept ballroom dancing for twenty years and lived out a fulfilling career representing Canada across the world with my now-husband for the past ten years.

During that time, I completed my undergraduate degree in business at McGill University, worked full-time for a few years, and then did an MBA at Concordia University. After that, I opened and ran my own business in Toronto for five years, eventually selling it to move back to Montreal and join SuccessFinder as the marketing lead.

As a Senior Director of Marketing & Communications, I've had the advantage of a varied background in dance, entrepreneurship, and business theory that I've been able to draw upon.

For example, colors that I know people are naturally drawn to for dance dresses are usually a hit when presented in the business world via branding. When I need to present to an internal team and help bring lively energy, I can pull from concepts that I know work: get people up and moving to some upbeat music with easy-to-follow movements, for example. When I set up a space in a business environment, like a booth for a conference or area of a corporate office, I rely on ideas from the dance world, mixing and matching colors and proportions, to guide me in creating visually appealing spaces.

To deliver business results, I trust my thousands of hours on the dance floor practicing, competing, and teaching, all while focusing on setting goals that are lofty enough to be motivational, and then putting in the work every day towards achieving them.

A key concept I learned in dance that serves me in business is to overprepare and practice so much that things become natural. Then, on the day of the actual performance, or in the business case, a presentation, you can stop thinking and lead with your heart.

When I reflect on how to best help my team, I dig into

what I saw worked in the dance world: each person must find their own style while developing a solid foundation of basic technical knowledge to allow for that freedom. You also need to find ways to connect with and motivate each person, keeping in mind that this is unique to every individual. How can we push the boundaries of current limits, physical or technical, a little more every day so that at the end of the year we see huge gains? Just like in the dance world, we strive to give stretch assignments where someone can try something new. Work on it alone for a while, and then get feedback to ensure alignment before getting back to self-development. There is nothing like doing something yourself and feeling it in your own body or mind to learn and retain the information.

Another element from the dance world that I take over to the professional context is regularly participating in multiday sessions. This is where you learn from someone new, get out of your usual environment (ideally with world-class experts), and push harder, both physically and mentally, for this sustained short period to see some real breakthroughs.

THE VISIONEER

Donna Syed
Kansas City, Kansas, USA

Donna's work as a professional development consultant, experiential innovation expert, and practitioner for a variety of neuro-rehab therapeutics focuses on high-performance development, neurodegenerative disorders, PTSD/mental health recovery, physical therapy, and innovative fitness approaches. Donna is also the author of Truthfairy Field Guide: No Guru Required.

Would you rather start learning quantum mechanics by watching two seasons of *The Muppet Show* or by sitting in a 1960s lecture hall for three hours every week for fifteen weeks at Princeton University?

Same learning targets, earning the same credit hours.

Personally, I would expect one to be reliably hilarious, relatable, and undoubtedly memorable; the other, intimidating, anxiety-producing, and intestinally disruptive. As prestigious as Princeton may be, it was Kermit the Frog who laid the foundation for my own education, and I think he and his friends could do a similar job delivering advanced physics.

How would I begin?

Gather six inquisitive first graders, an electrician, astrophysicist, cosmologist, and a handful of Jim Henson's magicians for a weekend at Skywalker Ranch (where they might also accidentally stumble upon the answers to Einstein's unfinished business).

In the time I have spent engaging physicists, technology wizards, writers, math teachers, fine artists, engineers, theater professionals, psychologists, mechanics, astronomers, musicians, physicians, athletes, religious people, architects, attorneys, professors, and great big businessmen—all of them, every single one of them— have the same glowing internal thread:

A driving desire to make things work through the lens of their focused interest.

As Brian explained, not all specialized professionals are innovators, but they are all creative problem solvers capable of doing what innovators do. Innovators are creative people who give themselves permission to draw from the ether, otherwise known as the land of All Things Possible. They dare to push the sky, asking for more twinkle from an already-fascinating star or a soft shower of meteors to glint over a Gulf shore aurora-swept horizon.

Innovators believe all is possible because they remember that everything we can now see and do was once just potential—until it existed. Anything that can be known, you can know. And if you don't see it, you can find it, often in the most unexpected places.

The truth is, innovators and visionary creatives are not long-bearded sorcerers or bibbidi-bobbidi-boo wand-wavers any more than physicists and PhDs are two-dimensional character actors (although, in my experience, they are most certainly characters of a most interesting sort). Although either could be found with the other engaging at a café over croissants and coffee on a Monday morning—you wouldn't necessarily notice them brewing magic if you weren't listening in.

The best-kept secret of the innovation process: It's more about letting go than endlessly kneading and pulling at your brain for a breakthrough idea. This is what usually causes the opposite, what I call Imagination Constipation (IC for short).

Remember, the treasures you have collected in your "filing cabinet" along the way hold recipes for magic— but to avoid discomfort, sometimes you just need to stop stirring for a little while.

What's in my magic filing cabinet?

Rich with impressions and experiences, my own magic filing cabinet is what makes my consulting work feel like a muse on vacation.

If you met me at the grocery store, you wouldn't notice that I think in equations, or that I deeply appreciate metaphor and irony, love to personify abstract ideas— and that my favorite sport is debilitating laughter. You probably wouldn't guess that reverse engineering and examining things upside down are among my favorite habits.

I don't look like the writer, costume designer, dance practitioner, gardener, or special education advocate that I am. You wouldn't know how many stages I've performed on, that I can change a car tire (or radiator) if necessary, or that I am a superfan of exactly one opera singer.

You couldn't guess that I indulge in architecture or neuroscience research, and it might surprise you that I can also speak fluent Hillbilly. From Sun Tzu to Einstein's sass and Tesla clapbacks, to classic Bugs Bunny and Mozart, I notice points of balance where there is contrast.

The best tuition I have ever paid has been with my attention, and the profits have come by engaging with the simplicity of inner-child curiosity. From fantastical nonfiction to the magical world of make-believe, it's all in there.

So, what comes of all this?

Well, all sorts of things. Here are a few:

- A Unified Theory of Divine Connectivity—a theoretical equation that connects the soul to its energy source, drawn from theology, mathematics, physics, biology, and network technology. You know, kind of like connecting to the Internet, using a cell phone, or sending a telepathic text message. When this inspiration landed, it was clear enough for me to begin writing an abstract that could be translated for anyone to understand—Sesame Street–style.

- Using a piece of wide rubber band, installed in just such a way to keep my classic car stereo connector from falling through the console's broken plastic, saving myself at least three hundred dollars and many days of silent driving. Ten years later, it's still solid—and practical.

- Comprehensive concept and collaborative design recommendations for the newly imagined lyric opera-ballet adaptation of a wildly famous modern fairytale.

- Orchestrating quartz crystal sound bath experiences for public stargazing events at astronomical observatories.

- Designing a $22 billion themed fascination park that will change the way human beings understand and engage our world — and one another. No suspended belief required.

True stories.

The next best-kept secret of Innovators: Pick up this book an hour before you must be somewhere important. Do you hear that? That's me laughing, wondering if talking about Innovation and Visioneering will interrupt or challenge your regular schedule the way it is known to do for many imaginative people.

No appointments today? Set a timer for ten minutes and try to perform a hotel-style cleaning on some deserving area of your home. You'll be lucky to finish the job before Inspiration will ask to enter the chat. "Big idea" updates that only need a "minute of your time" will leave you scrambling for a pen and anything to write on. Your bed might remain unmade.

You could also just rest. When you go to sleep, you could dream something fascinating and unexpected or solve the problem that has been mocking you all week.

Sound unreliable? If it seems like the timing could be bothersome, remember that it is your decision. You can ignore anything that occurs to you if you want to. It is also a tremendous gift to witness "big ideas" begin to breathe like the C&O #614 steam locomotive — her furnace full, patiently preparing for another majestic mountain haul.

While you're waiting for inspiration, it's a good idea for you to let off some steam, too.

Impatience with yourself is your greatest antagonist, and the opposite is also true. With this awareness, and your internal gears and levers engaged, the spectrum of potential for innovation is immeasurable.

Does this process drive me crazy? Not really, just as long as I remember to accept the reality of a cutting-room floor and to let go as much as I engage. There are only so many minutes each day our minds need to be (or should be) digging for treasure. Enjoying life as much as you enjoy this work is required to make your stay here (or anywhere) on Earth the best it can be.

My Sorcerer's Apprentice wish for you . . .

Be in awe. Tune in and unleash your imagination, curiosity, hope, and inspiration . . . and all the faith you can find in the yet-unseen. Dare to believe that all things are possible.

If you're reading this, you're invited — with the full permission you've been waiting for. The same permission Brian Collins offered when he invited me to join in this important work.

It's been a special kind of honor to describe what it's like to live a visioneering life — to invite others to ignite new frontiers with their own creative spark, to illuminate our world, to tell our stories, to encourage us to come full circle, to help us feel, envision, and create things that reflect the true and pure beauty of our world.

If you've been waiting, this is your Golden Ticket to wander around in the wonderous and infinite field of imagination and experience the alchemy of innovation.

PS Can you imagine Brian Collins as the lead writer for *The Muppet Show* series Quantum Mechanics reboot for Jim Henson Studios?

I can.

I can also imagine myself on that team — as the canary in the comedy coal mine.

Litmus test: Yeah, but did she fall on the floor laughing at least three times?

(Say when.)

THE NURSE

Carolyn E. Cole
Shingle Springs, California, USA

Carolyn's career began in nursing and has evolved into that of a COO in biotechnology, healthcare, and lifelong/long life learning.

It was my honor to attend Stanford University, where I was one of eighteen women accepted to the five-year class in the School of Nursing. I also received a degree (BA) in psychology by taking courses on the main campus, which was close to Stanford Hospital and the medical part of the campus.

From that foundation, I received a full traineeship from the National Institute of Mental Health (NIMH) to go to the Yale University School of Nursing. The faculty were interested in the cross-pollination I would bring during my two-year Master of Nursing Science (MSN) Program. I was asked to be one of three graduate students to build an innovative new subspecialty Psychiatric Liaison Nursing Program. The Yale University School of Medicine had such a program for physicians, and the Yale University of Nursing and the Yale New Haven Hospital saw the need for these nursing services to work alongside medicine to better meet the psychosocial needs of the patients. The cross-pollination prior to arriving in New Haven was accelerating with my joining a new world.

For the next ten years after graduating, I cross-pollinated the life I had been given to help all I could with the education, the training, and the expertise I had been privileged to receive.

As the healthcare industry changed, I saw it was necessary to learn about business. The Kellogg School of Management at Northwestern University was where I spent the next two years getting an MBA. Now I was using my nursing career background to cross-pollinate with the business school culture to learn marketing, strategy, management, organizational behavior and design, finance, and accounting. More understanding of complexity was required to manage complex systems both expanding and disintegrating with the progress of change. Cross-pollinating meant ongoing learning, mastery, and being courageous.

As different as the business world seemed at first, over time I realized that the same principles that worked in the medical field led to my being successful in the world of business. I used my nursing principles of assessment: research to collect needed information, assess resources, design a plan of action, implement the plan of action, and reassess/evaluate results. Repeat steps as needed. Also, use common sense and interpersonal skills, involve others, be honest, humble, and curious, learn from mistakes, persevere, have mental strength, keep learning, be resilient, never quit, and help others whenever possible.

For the next many years, I worked in industry, academia, biotechnology, and healthcare. I continued to live by my first nursing career principles to adapt to my next career.

I used the technique of cross-pollination as a strategy to create a whole new career shift to set myself up to work and lead many more years into the future. I envisioned a role that would allow me to bring all that I have lived and achieved to this point to help solve major challenges. Collaboration and teamwork with gifted others are essential to allow all kinds of new relationships, innovations, and creativity. Harnessing technology and big data in new teams of talent allows new possibilities of understanding, knowledge, and wisdom. I discovered that opportunity at a young start-up company. My title is Chief Operating Officer (COO), Biotechnology, Health, and Lifelong/Long Life Learning.

As before, I made use of the basic principles. However, I added a new strategy of making a point to encourage younger colleagues and friends to combine their expertise with mine to solve problems. Now I have extra wisdom to offer having learned from making mistakes in life, and I find many younger people eager to learn how to better live their life while helping us advance as a team.

In summary, Creative Cross-Pollination has been an essential technique and theme in my life and is extending out as a theme into the future. It has allowed flexibility in how I live and view the world. When challenges and obstacles appear, cross-pollination allows innovation and creativity to search for potential solutions, growth, and even survival.

THE ENTREPRENEUR

Greg Schumsky
San Diego, California, USA

Greg's creativity as an audiovisual director, scenic & exhibit designer, and creative engineer has allowed him to blend technical proficiency, artistic innovation, and leadership to deliver projects. His entrepreneurial passion is the development of Jackalope Junction, hopefully to be the world's first steampunk-Western family-friendly theme park, as well as a variety of other proprietary wholesome entertainment, including streaming content, books, and games.

When I was a young child, I had a desire to do many creative things—without knowing I had that desire. If my folks bought a movie camera, I wanted to get my hands on it and figure out how to use it. A film camera, same thing. Drawing, I'd need the biggest canvas I could find—a big wall behind our living room couch, to the chagrin (and anger) of my parents.

I was born to create, as I believe we all are. I didn't know what I truly wanted to be when I was about seven—but I knew I didn't want to be a fireman or policeman or have any other "normal" career. I was interested in being a filmmaker, working for Disney Imagineering or Jim Henson.

But at the same time, anything that brought smiles to people made me soar. So I was an animator, magician, and designer well into my adult years—I also loved audio production and so many more things. That all culminated with a new love called multimedia, where

I could combine sound and video with programming interactive stories.

That led to being a UX (user experience) designer—the art, more or less, of looking at ways to create the best possible experience for folks when using some software, an app, a website, or maybe even some device or electronic product. I believed that all people should be given a delightful experience when using something, whether for leisure or business. This then led to becoming a video game producer.

All of these things, as random as they may seem, helped me to adapt and redefine what I was doing through cross-pollination. It helped me reinvent my career numerous times to where I needed to be.

This allowed me to use all the things I loved to do (video, storytelling, audio production, animation, and programming—different skills or talents that led to where I am now) in the formation of taking what's been done already for so many years—theme parks—and creating something that's never been done. I call it Jackalope Junction, and it's the world's first steampunk-Western Storypark.

It's called a Storypark because it focuses completely on one story and will be presented not only as a physical space but a television series, books, and interactive media (most likely games), using all the things I did in the past to create something unthought of until now. The basis of the story of Jackalope Junction also uses cross-pollination, as it's taking two things I loved as a kid: the Western genre combined with the stories of Jules Verne.

Interestingly enough, both focus on taming the unknown or exploring unknown territories or places that could be filled with life-threatening danger—yet our heroes still pursue and persevere, despite the odds that come against them.

I want people, young and old alike, to not be afraid to push past their safe boundaries—to explore the unknown and take chances, despite the odds of failure or success. Be bold and brave. Don't be afraid to just try something and see what happens—and maybe that thing will lead to the next bigger thing. Sometimes it doesn't happen in a straight line or planned progression (or by any plan at all) but can seem quite random. Don't discount the random experiences you've had—you never know when a few of those will lead to some really great, wonderful idea that might just change the world.

10

Four
Creative
Cross-Pollination
Techniques

"Creativity is just connecting things."

—Steve Jobs

Now that you have gained insight into the concept of Creative Cross-Pollination, it's time to roll up your sleeves and have some fun putting it into practice. The four techniques I'll be presenting are both engaging and thought-provoking: Word Vines, Opposite Thinking, Spin Zones, and Traditional Open-Ended Stories. Each method offers a distinct approach to stimulating creativity, ensuring a dynamic and enriching experience whether you're embarking on this journey solo or with a collaborative team.

As you have hopefully realized by now, Creative Cross-Pollination is an expansive concept—one that is capable of manifesting in various forms and being executed through diverse methods. At times it emerges spontaneously, fueled by a sudden burst of imaginative inspiration, while in other instances it demands a deliberate and concentrated effort. The beauty of this process lies in its versatility and adaptability to different circumstances, making it a valuable asset in fostering innovation and generating fresh ideas.

With that in mind, these four techniques can serve as effective and powerful tools for facilitating Creative Cross-Pollination, either for yourself or your team. They may seem similar to techniques you already know of or have used before, and that's great, but hopefully now you will see them in perhaps a different light. As I mentioned from the start, Creative Cross-Pollination is something that we, as humans, have been doing since our friend Ug started drawing on cave walls. When you use these techniques or any others you may develop or have in your creativity "tool chest," hopefully Creative Cross-Pollination will supercharge them to deliver extraordinary results and a multitude of ideas!

On a related note, these four methods are designed to inject a sense of playfulness and exploration into the creative process, enhancing the potential for unique and groundbreaking outcomes. Remember Peter Pan Syndrome? By embracing these techniques, you open up avenues for collaboration, ideation, and problem-solving that extend beyond conventional boundaries.

I am confident that as you delve into these techniques you will discover not only the joy of the creative process but also the immense potential for innovation that lies within your grasp. Whether you're a lone explorer seeking inspiration or part of a collaborative team eager to break new ground, these techniques are bound to infuse excitement into your creative endeavors.

Word Vines

Word Vines, the first technique, involves cultivating ideas in a manner akin to the growth of vines, with words connecting and intertwining to form a rich tapestry of thoughts. Word Vines are a Creative Cross-Pollination technique I developed some time ago when I was looking for new ways to brainstorm a product variation. While they aren't appropriate for all situations (most techniques aren't), they work great when trying to brainstorm a new idea or concept. Here's how to create and use them:

Start by writing out what you're trying to ideate. Keep it to only two or three words. In the examples below, I decided to look for a new style of shorts and different ways to explain the concept of "increasing productivity." I set up either two or three columns, depending on the concept, and under each individual word, listed as many synonyms as I could think of. I then repeated the process, but this time listed antonyms.

Once you have as many words under each column as possible, the next step is to begin mixing and matching to create some new ideas that, in turn, will hopefully help spark that "big one" you're looking for.

While trying to think of ideas for a new style of shorts, some ideas might be a "premier category of cutoffs" or "retro out-of-fashion jeans." Different ways to think about increasing productivity might be "ginormous output" or "shrink the number of things."

These, of course, are just meant to be starting points to help you think of things differently.

New Style Shorts
Synonyms

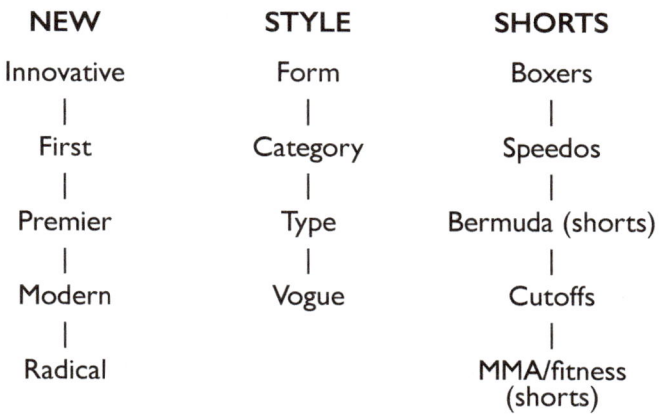

NEW	STYLE	SHORTS
Innovative	Form	Boxers
First	Category	Speedos
Premier	Type	Bermuda (shorts)
Modern	Vogue	Cutoffs
Radical		MMA/fitness (shorts)

New Style Shorts
Antonyms

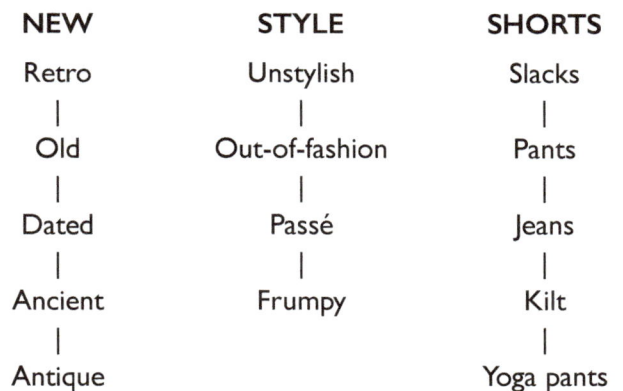

NEW	STYLE	SHORTS
Retro	Unstylish	Slacks
Old	Out-of-fashion	Pants
Dated	Passé	Jeans
Ancient	Frumpy	Kilt
Antique		Yoga pants

Increase Productivity
Synonyms

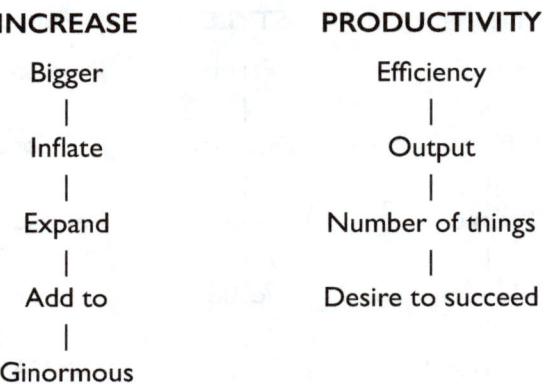

INCREASE	PRODUCTIVITY
Bigger	Efficiency
Inflate	Output
Expand	Number of things
Add to	Desire to succeed
Ginormous	

Increase Productivity
Antonyms

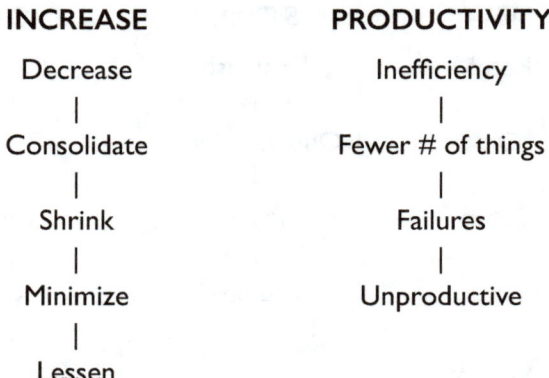

INCREASE	PRODUCTIVITY
Decrease	Inefficiency
Consolidate	Fewer # of things
Shrink	Failures
Minimize	Unproductive
Lessen	

Opposite Thinking

Opposite Thinking challenges traditional perspectives by encouraging you to explore the inverse of your initial ideas, paving the way for unconventional solutions. I've found Opposite Thinking to be a pretty good technique for ideas on how to extend a product's market or use.

Example 1

You sell car tires or have lots of used tires that you collect. What can you do with them if you have excess inventory, they are defective, or you just don't like the idea of them going into landfills?

Think about what your existing channels are. New tires might be sold to car dealerships, the general public, corporate fleets, etc. If used or defective, maybe they get picked up by waste disposal companies.

Now, time to get creative. Think about ways tires can be used in an "opposite way" than they were designed for. Another way to think about this would be, "What could be substituted with tires?" What about: playground equipment? Artificial mulch? Architectural features? Packing material? Insulation companies? Sound insulation?

Example 2

This may not be the most currently relevant product, but then again, I'm sure lots of companies and people have tons of CDs and DVDs stacked in a corner somewhere, and it provides a good example of Opposite Thinking. CDs and DVDs were the standard form of data storage for a long time. Technology has made them mostly obsolete, but I still have packages of unopened blanks at home. What if I owned a company that manufactured, sold, or used a lot of CDs and DVDs—you can only imagine the lost revenue as new storage systems rapidly emerged. Here's how Opposite Thinking could perhaps have helped with this dilemma.

Think about who traditionally bought blank CDs and DVDs: students, businesspeople, ad agencies, most companies, etc.

Now use Opposite Thinking to identify new users: artists, toy manufacturers, camping stores (survival mirrors . . .), etc.

Spin Zones

Spin Zones introduce an element of unpredictability, prompting you to navigate through unexpected twists and turns in your thought process. Although I've found Spin Zones particularly useful to identify potential new partnerships, synergies, or product extensions, like all these techniques, there are multiple scenarios they can be used for.

Generating Spin Zones has a lot to do with combining ideas.

Example 1

So let's take the idea of exploring new partnerships or synergies with your company. Say you want to do a special event or conference to attract new customers. (Note: this is different than new *partnerships* and *synergies*, which are the ultimate objectives here.)

Step one is to get the lay of the land and think about: Who is your market? Where do they hang out? Who do you want to attract? What do they read? What are their hobbies and interests? What benefits would they get from attending? What obstacles might prevent them from attending? What benefits can I offer to a potential partner?

Step two is to determine others who can help you reach your market. Be selfish — think of what you want to do and accomplish. Most important, get creative and think outside the box! You will do this by coming up with creative combinations — "Spin Zones."

For example, do you sell insurance? Have a "singles-only" seminar. Want to appeal to entrepreneurs or small business owners? Combine the idea of "swimming with the sharks" and "sales" by giving away tickets to the shark encounter at your local aquarium. Are you a pediatrician or orthodontist? Why not have an introductory event on-site at someplace like Chuck E. Cheese or Dave & Buster's? I think you get the idea.

Example 2

Another way to generate Spin Zones is to think like someone else. So many times when we are trying to generate ideas, we get stuck in our own paradigms, so this is a very simple but powerful technique that helps you or your team see things from a different perspective and can lead to really profound ideas!

Let's say you're an influencer known for your expertise of luxury items. To stay at the top of your game, you need to attract new followers, but how would you do that? Or let's say you're an engineer and you need to design a unique ride system. What about an artist looking to appeal to a broader market? How about a teacher looking for a new way to present lessons?

What ideas can you get by thinking about the perspectives that these types of individuals would have?

Police officer	Airline pilot
Elevator repairman	College professor
Computer programmer	Marine biologist
Soldier	Psychologist
Nanny	Farmer

So, using the examples I provided:

1. An influencer known for your expertise of luxury items looking to attract new followers.

    What kind of luxury items might a psychologist be interested in? High-end office accoutrements? Luxury writing instruments?

2. An engineer looking to design a unique ride system.

    Ideas from a pilot: flight simulators and trainers? Ideas from a farmer: planting patterns and techniques? Organic materials that can be incorporated?

3. An artist looking to appeal to a broader market.

   Ideas from an elevator repairman: interactive artwork with buttons and lights? What about a marine biologist? Maybe art that incorporates sand, shells, or even ocean trash?

4. A teacher looking for a new way to present lessons.

   How would a soldier do this? Perhaps by using a physical fitness exercise to explain how something works (physics, math, etc.)? What about a computer programmer? They may design a unique computer game.

You can spend a lot of time having fun with this one, coming up with different professions, each having its own perspective.

Traditional Open-Ended Stories

Talk about Creative Cross-Pollination and connecting the dots . . . Traditional Open-Ended Stories are a great way to harness the power of narrative to spark inspiration and cultivate imaginative thinking! It's a tried-and-true technique, but not used nearly enough for brainstorming, at least in my opinion. If you use the method I've facilitated for years, I virtually guarantee you and the participants will have so much fun and generate a ton of laughter in the room. Here's how I do it:

(Note: The objective for this example is to come up with new fashion products, but you can adapt it for other types of brainstorming objectives.)

1. Ask (ideally) six to eight people to volunteer to come up front.

2. Explain to them that they are going to be adding a single sentence to the story prompt you are about to deliver, thus continuing to build the story.

3. The rules are that there are no rules. As a matter of fact, you want to encourage them to come up with some crazy, silly, totally bizarre scenarios. (For the story below, it usually includes aliens and cows . . .)

4. Deliver the prompt below and go down the line, having each person add to the story.

    > Make sure the room you are in has either a dry-erase board or a large paper pad on an easel, and make sure you have colored markers.

    > Have the prompt written down in advance for all to see.

    > Again, the wording or objective can be modified to fit the objective of your brainstorm.

    > As you do this more often, you will get good at coming up with different story prompts. You can also find ideas online, but I always use this one because it's never failed to get great results:

You are representing the hottest new recording artist to come along in decades. She has decided that, in addition to performing, she wants to start her own clothing and accessory line.

But ... she wants some very unique products—things nobody else has. To make things even more interesting, she wants you to develop merchandise themed to the Old West. Yeehaw!

Your artist has been to Europe and seen some interesting stuff: clothes that glow, materials made from metals, even accessories made from old tires.

She has asked you to come up with a unique idea for either a new clothing concept or an interesting accessory. This is your big break. If you can't come through for her, you're fired!

Bling, you can do—cowboy boots are a different matter. You're thinking to yourself: "How am I going to come up with innovative new Western-themed products for this diva?!" I know—let's do an open-ended story! Here's how it begins:

"Back in the 1800s, when men were men, cows were cows, and the law of the land was the gun, there was a town called _____.

It was your typical Western town. Typical, that is, until that one fateful day when ..."

At this point, get the first person to come up with a fun name for the town and then add the first sentence. Go down the line and have each person contribute.

As each person adds their own twist to the story, write down their sentence. Make sure you remind and encourage them to go for funny and bizarre things!

When the story is completed, have everyone sit down. You then read the story back with much bravado.

Once the story has been read, usually to laughs and comments, it's time to begin the Creative Cross-Pollination process. At this point you want to encourage everyone to start throwing out ideas for new Western-themed products or accessories, no matter how strange or impractical, based on the contents from the story. If someone dreams up a cowboy hat with radar built into it for tracking aliens, that's fine. On the other hand, some ideas should be more practical as well. Perhaps a cowbell that glows in the dark because it is made of some kind of alien metal. The idea here is to get as many ideas as possible.

As the facilitator, your job is to help everyone connect those dots and write the ideas down. As the process progresses, you want to go through three stages. Think of the process as putting the ideas in a funnel. At the top is Stage 1 — all the crazy ideas everyone threw out. Even the cowboy hat with radar for tracking aliens. Stage 2 is getting people to start refining their ideas a bit more — things that are slightly more realistic. Some absurdity or silliness is still allowed. Perhaps a cowboy hat with GPS for precisely tracking aliens invading your ranch. Stage 3 is the time to get serious and come up with realistic ideas. These ideas can be far-reaching, which in many ways is the point, but they can be created or executed with current technology or systems and could potentially have a market. As unique as they might be, there could be a practical use.

At this stage ideas might include a cowboy hat with GPS sensors that pick up trackers attached to cattle, relaying information to other wearable tech or a smartphone app to warn ranchers immediately if cattle wander off-property. Maybe the hat delivers an audible tone or vibration to the rancher so they can be alerted right away. Could there be a real market for such a thing? I don't know, and you probably don't, either . . . but with additional research and focus groups, discussions with experts and ranchers—who knows? Maybe you are on to something! This is how taking an absurd story and leveraging Creative Cross-Pollination can deliver a novel idea. One of the great things about this technique is that it often delivers *many* novel ideas. Talk about serious play!

Flipping Over
to the
Bee-Side
of the Book

"I go from one area of the studio to another and gather pollen and sort of stimulate everybody."

—Walt Disney

A Special Word for Those Looking to Find a New or First Job—or Perhaps Reinvent Themselves

There's an old saying that if you find a job you love, you'll never work a day in your life. That's something I frequently tell students of all ages when I speak to them. It's so true. Maybe that's one reason in this day and age it seems like more people than ever are looking to reinvent their careers.

Perhaps you've gotten tired of your current career path, have been bitten by the entrepreneurial bug, or are finally at a place where you just want to follow your passion. Then again, it could be that you're looking to earn a little extra money, maybe to pay the rent or save up for that dream vacation. Maybe you're even trying to get that first "real job" of your career. Regardless of the reason, looking for a job is never easy. Trust me, I know. Been there, done that more than once—sometimes by choice, and sometimes not. Whatever your situation is, though, I wanted to share five personal thoughts about how I've used Creative Cross-Pollination to define new job opportunities. Hopefully these will help you think of ways to apply its concepts to your specific situation.

I've never defined my job search by looking at a specific industry.

For me, it's never been about wanting to work for a specific company or in a particular industry. It's always been about knowing what my skill set is and then matching those skills to a company or industry that interested me. I didn't grow up wanting to be an Imagineer. I wanted to be an astronaut. As I got older,

I realized and understood that I didn't have the skills to make that happen. But guess what company and job I *did* have the skills to pursue?

I've always taken the time to do a personal skills audit.

It's important to every so often take a personal skills assessment and think about not only what you're good at but if your skills are in line with where you want to go with your work. Our skills evolve over time. We get better at certain things, learn new things, and sometimes we realize we have skills we aren't particularly interested in using anymore. Also, realize that when I talk about skills, it's not only the hard ones, like driving a forklift or being an expert on Microsoft Excel, but also the important soft skills that you have. For example, communicating with others or managing people or projects — strengths that help us with our hobbies and interests. Were you in the drama club? Scouts? Do you sing in the shower? Don't forget to include these in your skill assessment. These are very important if you are looking to move in a new direction with your career, because often these are skills we've enjoyed using, but haven't had the opportunity to use in our professional life. Now may be the chance!

I've never been shy about reaching out.

Many people miss opportunities because they don't ask for them. On a related note, many people miss opportunities because they feel they aren't qualified. You should never be afraid to reach out to someone and ask for a chance to do a "meet and greet," grab some lunch, or otherwise connect. One thing I've learned as I've gotten older is that most people sincerely appreciate having someone show interest in their work, especially if they are trying to better themself. As a matter of fact, I can't remember a time when I was working for a company or as a consultant that I was turned away in this circumstance. It's a great way to open a door where one may not exist. Another excellent way to do this is to volunteer with an organization that interests you. Volunteering can help you gain new skills or sharpen existing ones . . . but until you reach out, you'll never get that chance.

I've always tried to find a way to connect to a job or company that interests me.

This is similar to my first point—that it's never been about wanting to work for a specific company or industry. However, once I do land in a job, I look for ways to make my work more interesting and personally fulfilling by cross-pollinating my skill set into an opportunity I'd like to pursue while still serving the company I'm working for. Remember how I said I always wanted to be an astronaut? Space has intrigued me ever since I was a little kid. If someone offered to stick me on a rocket ship, I'd blast off tomorrow. While I understand that probably isn't going to happen, I can tell you that when I was working as a video producer for a major media company, I convinced them it would be a good idea to shoot some stock footage of astronauts and space shuttle liftoffs while that was still happening. Sure enough, I made several trips to Cape Kennedy and not only got to see the magnificent spacecraft up close, but interview astronauts and go "behind the scenes" to many areas that would typically be off-limits during this amazing period of space history.

I've taken risks when it comes to getting attention and breaking through the "clutter."

I'm a big proponent of taking calculated risks in your job search and doing something creative to help you break through the clutter. When I graduated college with a degree in advertising and was trying to get my first job as a copywriter, I rigged my portfolio of writing samples to play music when it was open. (In an early version of professional Creative Cross-Pollination from my career, I took a sound chip out of a greeting card and used that to deliver the desired effect.) Later, when I was trying to get noticed by Walt Disney Imagineering after three rejections, I took a bolder approach. I'm going to preface this example by saying I wouldn't necessarily recommend this to anyone else . . . I knew it could have easily been the end of my Disney career before it ever began, but it was a risk I was willing to take. So, I went out and bought one of those traditional Mickey Mouse hats—you know, the black beanie with the ears. I ripped off one of the ears and crafted a ransom note. I actually cut out individual letters from magazines and newspapers. The note read something like "Want to be a Disney Imagineer. Am holding corporate symbol as hostage. Willing to negotiate." I then placed the ransom note with the severed ear in an envelope and sent it off. A bit dramatic? Certainly. But understanding the audience and having spoken to and built a relationship with the HR person I mailed it to, I took a calculated risk. Use good judgment, and perhaps a little more tact than I did, and you too might be able to break through the clutter.

Selected Bibliography

1. Amabile, Teresa. *Creativity in Context*. Avalon publishing, 1996.

2. Surrell, Jason. *The Haunted Mansion: From the Magic Kingdom to the Movies*. Rev. ed. Disney Editions, 2009.

3. Suddath, Claire. "A Brief History of: Velcro." Time, June 15, 2010. http://content.time.com/time/nation /article/0,8599,1996883,00.html.

Acknowledgments

This book is the culmination of a lifetime of experiences and acquaintances, all of which, and whom, would be impossible to acknowledge. That said, there are a few who stand out.

As a young kid, I remember my Aunt Jackie being one of the most supportive and creative people I knew. She was always writing and crafting stuff and even spent time in NYC making the rounds to a few ad agencies. Unfortunately, medical conditions kept Aunt Jackie from ever fulfilling her true potential, and she was taken far too early—but not before leaving a tremendous impression on me.

There are three others I need to thank. Jim Marra was my favorite instructor when I was an undergrad at Texas Tech University. At the time, he was a young PhD student teaching courses in creativity, so it's no wonder we clicked. He later went on to spend many years as a full professor at Temple University. Jim was the one who helped me believe I had the talent to make a living doing what I was passionate about—writing.

Once I got to Disney, I very quickly befriended a Cast Member who was about my age and working at the then-Disney-MGM Studios as a full-time Production Assistant. I started at the WDW Resort, checking in guests at the front desk of the Contemporary Resort, and Jerome Ravenna was the first person at Disney to help open doors for me. Without his friendship and support, I would have never had as many amazing opportunities as I did so early in my career, and boy, did we laugh a lot. Such a mensch!

Mike West was the person who hired a young kid with a quirky sense of humor into Imagineering. He and I shared the same punny sense of humor, and, again, I think it was being in the right place at the right time with the right skills. It couldn't have been money, because if I tried to write him a check and bribe my way in, it would have bounced. Whatever he saw in me, I'm eternally grateful to Mike for starting me on the ride of my life — one that I still haven't exited.

On the family side of things, my older brother, Steve, who to this day pulls the "You know you were adopted" line, always had the coolest and most eclectic set of interests. He's the one most responsible for filling my mental filing cabinet as a kid. From magic to science fiction, Indian food and other exotic cuisines, Eastern beliefs and cultures . . . I could go on. Steve introduced me to so much stuff growing up. All these years later he still does, and next to my parents, has been my biggest cheerleader and supporter throughout my life.

Speaking of my parents — wow! Did I hit the jackpot. Both have passed now, but my attorney dad and travel agent mom were just the absolute best. They were always encouraging and humored my brother's and my whims, even when we traveled with them to Mexico City as young teenagers and wanted to try "do-it-yourself bullfighting" at Cortijo La Morena in Texcoco. Seriously. Later, when I worked as an Imagineer, I'm not sure they actually understood what I did, but they knew I was happy, and that was all that mattered.

To my incredible wife, whose unwavering support and encouragement fuel my creativity every day. Poor Tina, having to put up with the kid in me. She's not even a fan of theme parks — or at least the crowds — but she's a fan of me and has stood by in tough times and good ones. I simply can't ask for a better partner to spin around the Earth with!

To my kids, Cameron, Kyle, and Carly, I've had to apologize several times for having a dad like me. I couldn't ask for better kids and they make me proud every single day. They too, like Tina, put up with the kid in me and make my life so full and so much fun. I've told them plenty of times that when I'm gone, I'm coming back to haunt and taunt them as much as I can!

Finally, to my colleagues and collaborators, whose insights and contributions helped shape this work — it is as much yours as it is mine. And to all the cross-pollinators of the world — the thinkers, the dreamers, the boundary-breakers — keep connecting ideas, challenging the status quo, having fun, and making the world a more innovative place. After all, this book is for you.

About the Author

A former Walt Disney Imagineer, Brian helped create the magic for virtually all of Disney's Florida theme parks. As a master storyteller, he engaged in a variety of creative development projects including writing scripts and spiels for some of the world's most beloved attractions. However, his depth of expertise reaches well beyond the realm of pixie dust, fairy tales, and delivering world-class entertainment.

Over the course of his fascinating career, Brian has produced work for a who's-who list of corporations as well as small entrepreneurial ventures. He is an expert on immersive experiences and environments. This, combined with his love and deep understanding of new and emerging technologies and, most importantly, how they apply to business, entertainment, education, and beyond, is the trademark of his work. Given this, a "normal" day for him might include exploring augmented reality, synthetic environments, generative AI, holograms, haptics, or some other exotic "sci-fi" tech that's out there . . . or on the way.

A passionate educator, Brian was a founding member of the Central Florida STEM Education Council. He has served on the faculty at several schools and is currently a full-time instructor at the University of Central Florida, where he teaches a variety of courses related to theme park, experiential, attraction, and event design to the next generation. He is also a cofounder of the Ensō Education Institute, a think tank designed to explore ways that education can be improved, transformed, and disrupted. In addition to his academic and educational work, he is a sought-after innovation consultant through his practice known as The Brainstorm Institute.

Brian's remarkable career has been built on three diverse yet interconnected pillars: Innovation, Education, and Emerging Technologies. Drawing on expertise from any one, or all three, this dynamic fusion has fueled his work and allowed him to deliver unique and exciting solutions to a wide variety of global clients and verticals, including entertainment, consumer products, military, and much more. Brian also serves on the advisory boards of various tech-based start-ups, further solidifying his position at the forefront of innovation. He is an accomplished speaker and has graced stages across the globe. His presentations have captivated audiences in Canada, Denmark, the Netherlands, Mexico, Dubai, Japan, and beyond.

In addition to The Brainstorm Institute, Brian formed WDWithMe.com to further leverage his background as a Disney Imagineer. He has a large social media following, is often interviewed on podcasts, and is a former columnist for *WDW Magazine*.

Brian earned his master's degree in marketing from Webster University, where he was a Distinguished Graduate. His Bachelor of Arts degree in advertising was awarded by Texas Tech University. He was also an officer in the United States Air Force auxiliary (Civil Air Patrol), qualified in aerial photography and air search and rescue, and previously served as the FL Wing's Director of Aerospace Education.

On a personal note, Brian is active in his synagogue, claims to be a heck of a good cook, and loves Belgian chocolate . . . but then again, who doesn't?

About the Illustrator

Nico Gigante is the talented and visionary artist whose illustrations appear throughout *Creative Cross-Pollination*. His work brings imagination to life across the worlds of film, themed entertainment, and visual storytelling. Nico's experience spans multiple industries, and he specializes in graphic design, illustration, background painting, and concept art. His portfolio includes everything from immersive theme park signage to richly detailed concept art for award-winning short films—each piece infused with his own style of wonder, precision, and narrative depth.

Nico's mastery of Adobe Creative Suite, particularly Photoshop and Illustrator, is matched by his fluency in traditional illustration and digital painting techniques. This rare blend of technical skill and artistic intuition allows him to adapt seamlessly to a wide range of creative challenges, making him a sought-after collaborator for projects that demand both beauty and clarity.

His contribution to *Creative Cross-Pollination* is a testament to his creative range and storytelling power. The illustrations he crafted for the book are not just visually striking—they're conceptually rich, enhancing the themes of imagination, exploration, and transformation that define the work. Nico's ability to translate abstract ideas into compelling visuals helped shape the book's identity, making each chapter a fun and vibrant experience for readers.

Beyond his professional work, Nico is a passionate observer of the world. He finds inspiration in travel, often sketching scenes in ink from bustling streets or quiet corners. Whether he's chasing tacos after a soccer match or keeping up with his energetic puppy, Nico brings a sense of playfulness and curiosity to everything he does—qualities that shine through in his art.

To explore more of Nico's work or to connect for future collaborations, visit www.nicodraws.com and follow him on Instagram: @gigantenico.

www.ingramcontent.com/pod-product-compliance
Lightning Source LLC
Chambersburg PA
CBHW061803120626
46550CB00005B/2116

* 9 7 8 1 9 6 0 8 8 1 0 7 6 *